THE AUSTRALIAN Women's Weekly

VEGETARIAN

for everyone

TRIPLE TESTED
THE AUSTRALIAN WOMEN'S WEEKLY · TEST KITCHEN

WE TEST ALL
OUR RECIPES | 3 TIMES

Our team of chefs at The Australian Women's Weekly Test Kitchen are developing and testing recipes daily to make sure every one you make at home is a success. We are located right in the heart of Sydney, Australia.

CONTENTS

SUMMER VEGETABLES

ASPARAGUS

AVOCADOS

BEANS, BUTTER; GREEN; FLAT; SNAKE

CAPSICUM (BELL PEPPER)

CELERY

CHILLIES

CHOKO (CHAYOTE)

CORN

CUCUMBER

EGGPLANT

LETTUCE

OKRA

ONIONS, GREEN (SCALLIONS); SPRING

PEAS, SUGAR SNAP

POTATOES

RADISH

SQUASH

TOMATOES

WATERCRESS

ZUCCHINI

AUTUMN VEGETABLES

ASIAN GREENS

AVOCADOS

BEANS

BROCCOLI

BRUSSELS SPROUTS

CABBAGE

CAPSICUM (BELL PEPPER)

CARROTS

CAULIFLOWER

CELERY

CELERIAC (CELERY ROOT)

CHESTNUTS

CHOKO (CHAYOTE)

CORN

CUCUMBER

EGGPLANT

FENNEL

GINGER

KUMARA (ORANGE SWEET POTATO)

LEEK

LETTUCE

MUSHROOMS

OKRA

ONIONS

PARSNIP

POTATOES

PUMPKIN

SHALLOTS

SILVER BEET (SWISS CHARD)

SPINACH

TOMATOES

TURNIPS

WITLOF (BELGIAN ENDIVE)

ZUCCHINI

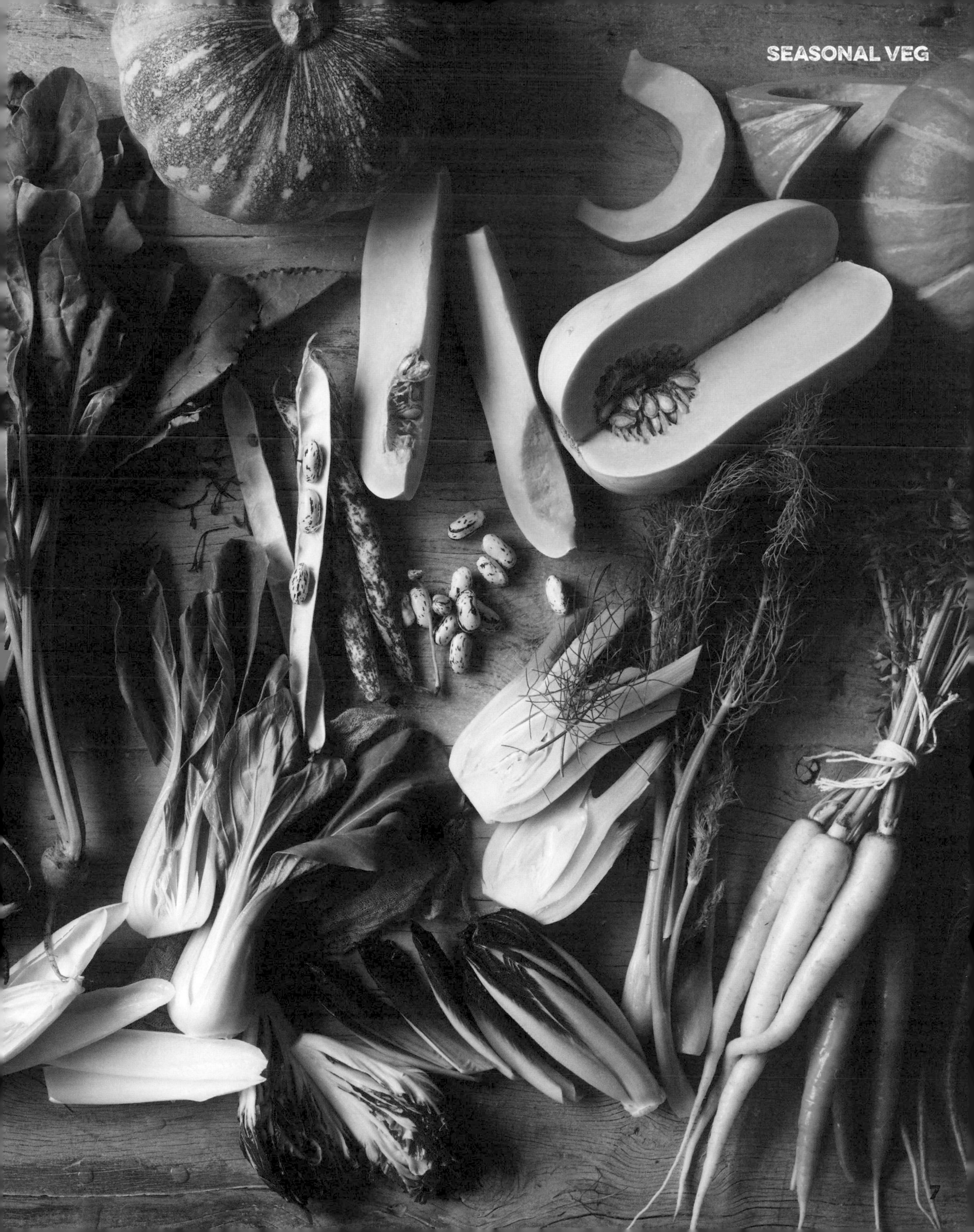

WINTER VEGETABLES

AVOCADOS

BEETROOT (BEETS)

BROCCOLI

BRUSSELS SPROUTS

CABBAGE

CARROTS

CAULIFLOWER

CELERIAC (CELERY ROOT)

CELERY

FENNEL

JERUSALEM ARTICHOKES (SUNCHOKES)

KOHLRABI

KUMARA (ORANGE SWEET POTATO)

LEEK

OKRA

OLIVES

ONIONS

PARSNIP

POTATOES

PUMPKIN

SILVER BEET (SWISS CHARD)

SPINACH

SWEDE

TURNIPS

WITLOF (BELGIAN ENDIVE)

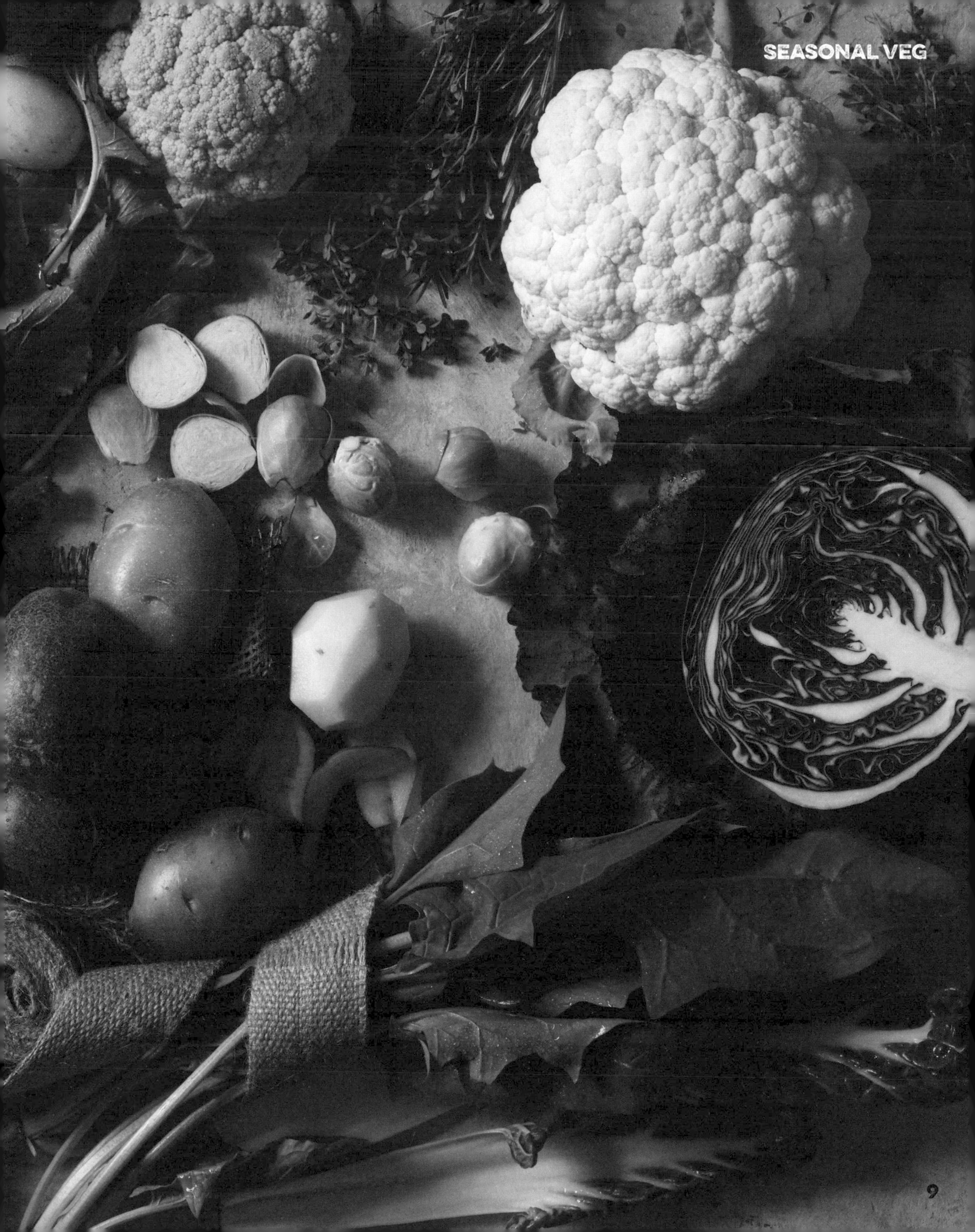

SPRING VEGETABLES

ARTICHOKES, GLOBE

ASIAN GREENS

ASPARAGUS

AVOCADOS

BEANS, BROAD (FAVA); GREEN

BEETROOT (BEETS)

BROCCOLI

CARROTS

CAULIFLOWER

CHILLIES

CORN

CUCUMBER

GARLIC

LETTUCE

MUSHROOMS

ONIONS, GREEN (SCALLIONS); SPRING

PEAS

POTATOES

SILVER BEET (SWISS CHARD)

SPINACH

TOMATOES

WATERCRESS

ZUCCHINI

ZUCCHINI FLOWERS

LUNCHES & SNACKS

KALE & WALNUT TARTS

PREP + COOK TIME 1 HOUR 20 MINUTES SERVES 6

40g (1½ ounces) butter, melted

2½ cups (310g) LSA (see Notes)

2 free-range eggs

30g (1 ounce) baby kale leaves, chopped finely

⅓ cup (35g) chopped roasted walnuts

⅔ cup (160g) ricotta, crumbled

4 free-range eggs, extra

1⅓ cups (330ml) milk

2 teaspoons finely grated lemon rind

2 cloves garlic, crushed

2 teaspoons finely chopped fresh tarragon

60g (2 ounces) snow pea tendrils

1 tablespoon lemon juice

1 tablespoon olive oil

1 Preheat oven to 200°C/400°F. Brush six 10cm (4-inch) loose-based fluted tart tins with half the melted butter. Place tins on an oven tray.

2 Combine LSA, eggs and remaining melted butter in a medium bowl; season. Press LSA mixture onto base and side of tins. Bake for 10 minutes; set aside to cool. Reduce oven to 160°C/325°F.

3 Place kale, walnuts and ricotta in tart cases. Whisk extra eggs, milk, rind, garlic and tarragon in a large jug until combined; season. Pour egg mixture over filling.

4 Bake tarts for 30 minutes or until just set. Leave tarts in tins for 5 minutes to cool slightly, but while still warm, remove from tins (see Notes).

5 Meanwhile, combine snow pea tendrils, juice and oil in a small bowl; season to taste.

6 Serve tarts topped with snow pea tendrils.

Test Kitchen
NOTES

LSA is a ground linseed, sunflower seed and almond mixture that can be found at supermarkets and health food stores.

You must remove the tarts from the tins while they are still warm to prevent them from sticking.

EGGPLANT PARMIGIANA 'MEATBALL' SUBS

PREP + COOK TIME 1 HOUR SERVES 6

1 medium eggplant (300g), peeled, chopped coarsely

2 tablespoons olive oil

400g (12½ ounces) canned chickpeas (garbanzo beans), drained, rinsed

1 small red onion (100g), chopped finely

2 cloves garlic, crushed

1 tablespoon finely chopped fresh rosemary leaves

1 cup (80g) finely grated parmesan

1½ cups (150g) packaged breadcrumbs

vegetable oil, for deep-frying

6 long soft bread rolls (300g)

1 cup (260g) tomato pasta sauce

¾ cup (60g) finely grated parmesan, extra

40g (1½ ounces) baby rocket (arugula) leaves

2 teaspoons balsamic vinegar

1 Preheat oven to 200°C/400°F. Line an oven tray with baking paper.

2 Place eggplant on tray; drizzle with olive oil. Roast for 25 minutes or until golden and tender.

3 Process eggplant, chickpeas, onion, garlic, rosemary and parmesan until combined; season. Add 1 cup breadcrumbs; pulse until combined. Roll level tablespoons of eggplant mixture into 24 balls. Roll eggplant balls in remaining breadcrumbs to coat.

4 Heat vegetable oil in a wok or large saucepan; deep-fry eggplant balls, in batches, for 2 minutes or until golden and heated through. Drain on paper towel.

5 Preheat grill (broiler). Cut rolls lengthways from the top, without cutting all the way through. Spread sides with sauce; top with 4 eggplant balls and sprinkle with extra parmesan. Grill for 2 minutes or until cheese melts.

6 Combine rocket and vinegar in a small bowl; divide salad between subs.

CAULIFLOWER 'PIZZA' WITH MOZZARELLA & ZUCCHINI

PREP + COOK TIME 1 HOUR 25 MINUTES SERVES 4

1 small cauliflower (1kg), trimmed, cut into florets

¼ cup (30g) coarsely grated cheddar

1 free-range egg, beaten lightly

¾ cup (60g) coarsely grated parmesan

½ cup (130g) tomato passata

2 small zucchini (180g), sliced thinly into ribbons

1 cup fresh basil leaves

1 fresh small red (serrano) chilli, sliced thinly

100g (3 ounces) buffalo mozzarella, torn coarsely

1 tablespoon olive oil

1 tablespoon finely grated lemon rind or strips (see Notes)

1 tablespoon lemon juice

1 Preheat oven to 200°C/400°F. Line two oven trays with baking paper; mark a 22cm (8¾-inch) round on paper, turn paper over.

2 Process cauliflower until finely chopped. Place in a microwave safe bowl, cover with plastic wrap; microwave on HIGH (100%) for 12 minutes or until tender. (Alternatively steam cauliflower, but do not boil it as this will make the crust too soggy). Drain. When cool enough to handle, place cauliflower in the centre of a clean tea towel. Gather ends together, then squeeze excess moisture from cauliflower.

3 Combine cauliflower, cheddar, egg and ¼ cup of the parmesan in a large bowl; season. Shape cauliflower mixture into marked rounds on trays; smooth the surface. Bake for 25 minutes or until golden.

4 Spread bases with passata, half each of the zucchini and basil, then chilli, mozzarella and remaining parmesan. Bake for 20 minutes or until golden and crisp.

5 Meanwhile, combine oil, rind, juice and remaining zucchini and basil in a medium bowl; season to taste.

6 Serve pizzas topped with zucchini salad.

Passata is sieved tomato puree sold alongside other bottled pasta sauces in most supermarkets. You can use your favourite pasta sauce instead, if you prefer.

If you have one, use a zester to create strips of lemon rind. If you don't have one, peel two long, wide strips of rind from the lemon, without the white pith, then cut them lengthways into thin strips.

Test Kitchen NOTES

Beetroot relish makes about 1½ cups. Store leftover relish, covered, in the fridge for up to 2 weeks. Beetroot relish goes well with cheese or in burgers and sandwiches.

If pomegranate molasses is not available, combine 1 tablespoon balsamic vinegar and 1 tablespoon caster (superfine) sugar.

TEMPEH BLAT SANDWICH

PREP + COOK TIME 1 HOUR MAKES 4

1 medium avocado (250g), chopped coarsely

1 tablespoon lemon juice

8 slices sourdough bread (360g), toasted

¼ cup (75g) whole-egg mayonnaise

½ teaspoon ground turmeric

1 medium tomato (150g), sliced thinly

1 medium carrot (120g), cut into matchsticks

40g (1½ ounces) baby rocket (arugula) leaves

TEMPEH BACON

2 tablespoons tamari

1 tablespoon olive oil

1 tablespoon pure maple syrup

1 teaspoon smoked paprika

300g (9½ ounces) tempeh, cut into 1cm (½-inch) slices

BEETROOT RELISH

3 medium beetroot (500g), grated coarsely

1 shallot (25g), chopped finely

2 tablespoons pomegranate molasses (see Notes)

1 teaspoon ground allspice

1 teaspoon coriander seeds, crushed

2 tablespoons red wine vinegar

½ cup (125ml) water

1 tablespoon olive oil

1 Make tempeh bacon.

2 Meanwhile, make beetroot relish.

3 Combine avocado and juice in a small bowl; season.

4 Place 4 slices of bread on a board; spread with combined mayonnaise and turmeric. Top with tomato, tempeh bacon, carrot, avocado mixture, rocket and beetroot relish. Top with remaining slices of bread.

TEMPEH BACON Preheat oven to 200°C/400°F. Line an oven tray with baking paper. Combine tamari, oil, maple syrup and paprika in a medium bowl. Add tempeh; toss to coat. Place tempeh, in a single layer, on tray. Bake for 20 minutes, turning halfway through cooking, until crisp.

BEETROOT RELISH Place ingredients, except oil, in a small saucepan over high heat. Reduce heat; simmer, uncovered for 10 minutes or until thickened. Stir in oil; cool.

BAKED VEGETABLE CRISPS

PREP + COOK TIME

1 HOUR 30 MINUTES

SERVES 2

Preheat oven to 150°C/300°F. Line three oven trays with baking paper, then coat with cooking oil spray; sprinkle with sea salt flakes. Using a mandoline or V-slicer, cut 1 large (180g) carrot, 1 large (180g) purple carrot and 1 medium (250g) parsnip lengthways into paper-thin slices. Place vegetables in a single layer on trays. Spray with cooking oil; sprinkle with a little more sea salt flakes (or one of the seasoning variations opposite). Bake for 1¼ hours or until crisp; cool.

SUMAC & THYME

1 teaspoon sumac and 2 teaspoons chopped fresh thyme.

FENNEL & CHILLI

Grind 2 teaspoons fennel seeds with a pestle and mortar until coarsely ground; stir in 1 teaspoon dried chilli flakes.

SMOKED PAPRIKA

1 teaspoon smoked paprika.

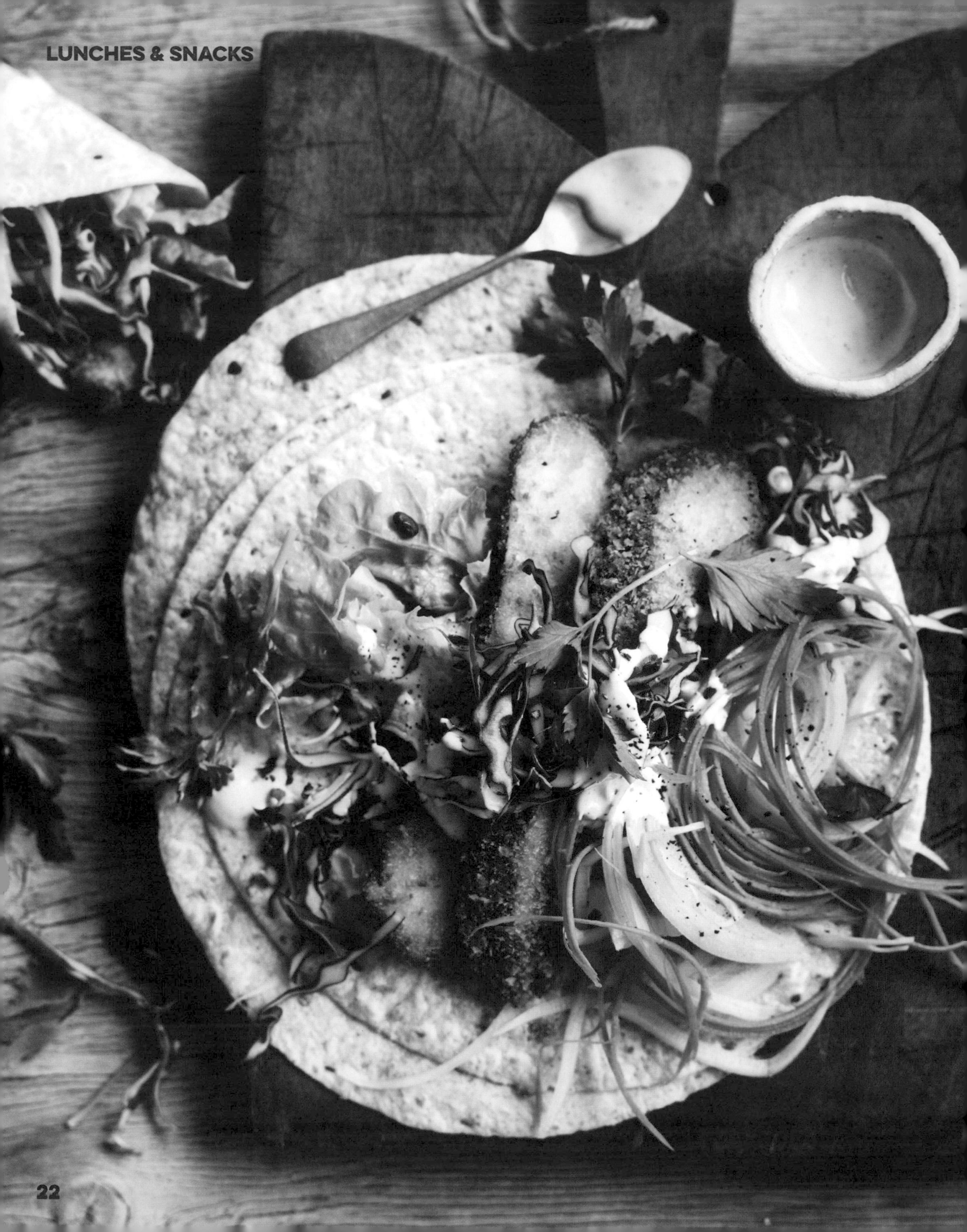

CRUMBED ZUCCHINI & SLAW WRAPS

PREP + COOK TIME 40 MINUTES SERVES 4

2 medium zucchini (240g), sliced thinly, lengthways

2 free-range eggs, beaten lightly

1⅓ cups (200g) panko (japanese) breadcrumbs

¼ cup (60ml) olive oil

1 green oak leaf lettuce, leaves separated

4 x 20cm (8-inch) wholegrain wraps (70g)

WHITE BARBECUE SAUCE

¼ teaspoon garlic powder

¼ teaspoon cayenne pepper

2 teaspoons horseradish cream

⅓ cup (100g) whole-egg mayonnaise

1 tablespoon lemon juice

1 tablespoon water

SLAW

1 cup (80g) finely shredded red cabbage

½ small white onion (40g), sliced thinly

1 medium carrot (120g), grated coarsely

⅔ cup (50g) crunchy sprout combo

1 Make white barbecue sauce, then the slaw.

2 Dip zucchini in egg, then coat in breadcrumbs, pressing lightly to secure.

3 Heat half the oil in a large frying pan over medium-high heat; cook half the zucchini for 3 minutes or until both sides are golden and tender. Repeat with remaining oil and zucchini.

4 Place lettuce along centre of each wrap; top evenly with slaw, zucchini and remaining white barbecue sauce. Roll to enclose filling.

WHITE BARBECUE SAUCE Stir ingredients in a small bowl.

SLAW Place cabbage, onion, carrot, sprouts and half the white barbecue sauce in a medium bowl; toss to combine. Season to taste.

ROASTED STICKY TOFU BUNS

PREP + COOK TIME 45 MINUTES (+ STANDING) SERVES 4

300g (9½ ounces) firm tofu

1 teaspoon smoked paprika

1½ tablespoons tomato sauce (ketchup)

1½ tablespoons smokey barbecue sauce

¼ cup (60ml) soy sauce

¼ cup (60ml) rice wine vinegar

2 tablespoons brown sugar

1 lebanese cucumber (130g), sliced thinly lengthways

1 large carrot (180g), sliced thinly lengthways

1 fresh long red chilli, sliced thinly on the diagonal

1 tablespoon caster (superfine) sugar

2 tablespoons rice wine vinegar, extra

4 fresh coriander (cilantro) sprigs

1 tablespoon coarsely chopped roasted salted peanuts

4 small soft white bread rolls (520g), split

1 Preheat oven to 200°C/400°F. Grease and line an oven tray with baking paper.

2 Place tofu on a plate lined with paper towel. Top with another plate; stand for 10 minutes. Cut tofu crossways into eight slices, rub with paprika; season.

3 Bring sauces, vinegar and sugar to a simmer in a small saucepan over medium heat. Simmer for 3 minutes or until thickened slightly. Pour sauce mixture over tofu; turn to coat. Transfer tofu to tray; bake for 20 minutes, basting occasionally with sauce mixture or until tofu is golden.

4 Combine cucumber, carrot, chilli, sugar and extra vinegar in a medium bowl; stand for 10 minutes or until vegetables soften. Drain.

5 Place tofu, pickled vegetables, coriander and nuts between rolls.

NOTE This recipe can easily be doubled or tripled to feed more people.

You will need four 2 cup (500ml) heatproof jars with fitted lids for this recipe.

ASIAN NOODLE SOUP IN A JAR

PREP + COOK TIME 20 MINUTES SERVES 4

4 hard-boiled free-range eggs, halved

1 tablespoon vegetarian tom yum paste

40g (1½ ounces) dried rice vermicelli noodles

8 oyster mushrooms (90g), torn

4 x 5cm (2-inch) long strips thinly sliced fresh ginger

4 fresh kaffir lime leaves, torn

8 cherry tomatoes, halved

⅓ cup (25g) bean sprouts

1 fresh long red chilli, sliced thinly

1 lime (65g), quartered

1.5 litres (6 cups) boiling water (see Notes)

¼ cup fresh coriander (cilantro) leaves

1 Divide eggs, paste, noodles, mushrooms, ginger, lime leaves, tomatoes, sprouts and chilli among four 2 cup (250ml) heatproof jars. Squeeze a lime quarter over ingredients in each jar; add lime to jars.

2 Pour 1½ cups (375ml) of the boiling water into each jar; stand, uncovered, for 6 minutes or until noodles are tender. Stir ingredients together. Serve topped with coriander.

Test Kitchen NOTES

This recipe is perfect to take to work. Add more or less tom yum paste to taste.

You can use boiling vegetable stock instead of boiling water for extra flavour.

CARROT & HARISSA FALAFEL WITH TAHINI YOGHURT

PREP + COOK TIME 1 HOUR SERVES 4

2 medium carrots (240g), grated coarsely

400g (12½ ounces) canned chickpeas (garbanzo beans), drained, rinsed

1 small red onion (100g), chopped finely

1 teaspoon ground cumin

1 tablespoon harissa

¼ cup plain (all-purpose) flour

½ teaspoon baking powder

1 free-range egg

1½ cups (225g) panko (japanese) breadcrumbs

vegetable oil, for deep-frying

150g (4½ ounces) green beans, trimmed, halved lengthways

2 baby cos (romaine) lettuce (360g), leaves separated

1 lebanese cucumber (130g), sliced thinly

¼ cup fresh flat-leaf parsley leaves

2 teaspoons lemon rind strips (see Notes)

TAHINI YOGHURT

1 small clove garlic, crushed

2 tablespoons lemon juice

2 tablespoons tahini

¾ cup (200g) greek-style yoghurt

1 tablespoon shredded fresh flat-leaf parsley

1 Process carrot, chickpeas, onion, cumin, harissa, flour, baking powder and egg until mixture just comes together; season. Transfer mixture to a large bowl; stir in ¾ cup of the breadcrumbs. Roll level tablespoons of carrot mixture into balls (mixture should make about 28). Roll falafel in remaining breadcrumbs to coat.

2 Fill a large saucepan or wok one-third with oil and heat to 180°C/350°F (or until a cube of bread browns in 15 seconds). Deep-fry falafel, in batches, for 2 minutes or until golden and cooked through. Drain on paper towel.

3 Meanwhile, make tahini yoghurt.

4 Boil, steam or microwave beans until just tender; drain. Rinse under cold water; drain.

5 Combine lettuce, cucumber and beans in a large bowl. Serve salad topped with falafel and tahini yoghurt; sprinkle with parsley and lemon rind.

TAHINI YOGHURT Combine ingredients in a small bowl; season to taste.

Test Kitchen NOTES

If you have one, use a zester to create the strips of lemon rind. If you don't have one, peel two long, wide strips of rind from the lemon, without the white pith, then cut them lengthways into thin strips.

CARROT, FETTA & QUINOA TARTS

PREP + COOK TIME 45 MINUTES SERVES 8

400g (12½ ounces) baby (dutch) carrots, unpeeled

150g (4½ ounces) fresh ricotta

100g (3 ounces) fetta, crumbled

1 clove garlic, crushed

1 egg

¼ teaspoon fennel seeds

¼ teaspoon cumin seeds

¼ cup (20g) finely grated parmesan

2 tablespoons extra virgin olive oil

1 cup (280g) greek-style yoghurt

½ cup snow pea tendrils

QUINOA DOUGH

1⅔ cups (250g) plain (all-purpose) flour

¼ cup (50g) red quinoa

½ teaspoon dried yeast

1 teaspoon flaked sea salt

⅓ cup (80ml) extra virgin olive oil

⅔ cup (160ml) hot water

1 Make quinoa dough.

2 Preheat oven to 220°C/425°F.

3 Trim carrot tops, leaving 2cm (¾-inch) stem attached; reserve a small handful of the tops. Wash carrots and tops. Finely chop carrot tops; you'll need 2 tablespoons. Combine chopped carrot tops with ricotta, fetta, garlic and egg in a medium bowl. Season.

4 Divide the dough in half. Roll out one half of the dough on a piece of lightly floured baking paper into a 12cm x 40cm (4½-inch x 16-inch) oval. Lift paper and dough onto a large oven tray. Repeat with remaining pastry and a second tray.

5 Spread each oval with half the cheese mixture; top with carrots. Sprinkle with seeds and parmesan; drizzle with oil, season.

6 Bake tarts for 25 minutes or until pastry is golden and cooked through. Serve tart slices topped with spoonfuls of yoghurt and snow pea tendrils.

QUINOA DOUGH Place ingredients, except the hot water in a food processor; pulse for a few seconds until combined. With motor operating, add the water; process for 3 minutes until well combined. Form dough into a ball; wrap in plastic wrap. Set aside.

GREEN QUINOA WITH SESAME EGGS

PREP + COOK TIME 25 MINUTES SERVES 2

1 cup (250g) vegetable stock

½ cup (100g) white quinoa, rinsed

4 eggs, at room temperature

2 teaspoons coconut oil

1 small clove garlic, crushed

1 fresh small red chilli, sliced thinly

2 cups (80g) thinly sliced kale (see Notes)

2 cups (90g) firmly packed, thinly sliced silver beet (swiss chard) (see Notes)

1 tablespoon lemon juice

¼ cup finely chopped fresh flat-leaf parsley

1 tablespoon white sesame seeds

1 tablespoon black sesame seeds

1 teaspoon sea salt flakes

1 Place stock and quinoa in a medium saucepan; bring to the boil. Reduce heat to low-medium; simmer gently for 15 minutes or until most of the stock is absorbed. Remove from heat; cover, stand 5 minutes.

2 Meanwhile, cook eggs in a small saucepan of boiling water for 5 minutes. Remove immediately from boiling water; cool under running cold water for 30 seconds.

3 Heat coconut oil in a medium saucepan over medium heat. Add garlic and chilli; cook stirring, for 2 minutes or until fragrant. Add kale and silver beet; stir until wilted. Add cooked quinoa and juice; season to taste.

4 Combine parsley, both sesame seeds and salt in a small bowl. Peel eggs; roll in parsley mixture.

5 Serve quinoa topped with eggs.

Test Kitchen NOTES

You will need to buy 1 bunch kale and 1 bunch silver beet (swiss chard).

Leftover greens can be wilted in a little olive oil or chopped and added to soups.

LENTIL SAUSAGE ROLLS WITH TOMATO SUMAC SALAD

PREP + COOK TIME 45 MINUTES SERVES 4

2 x 400g (12½ ounces) canned lentils, drained, rinsed

1 small brown onion (80g), grated finely

2 cloves garlic, crushed

⅓ cup (45g) coarsely chopped, roasted pistachios

1 teaspoon sweet paprika

1 teaspoon ground cumin

¼ teaspoon ground cinnamon

¼ teaspoon dried chilli flakes

1 free-range egg, beaten lightly

10 sheets fillo pastry

cooking oil spray

½ teaspoon sumac

⅔ cup (190g) greek-style yoghurt

TOMATO SUMAC SALAD

200g (6½ ounces) mixed baby tomatoes, chopped

½ small red onion (50g), sliced thinly

1 tablespoon thinly sliced preserved lemon rind

100g (3 ounces) mesclun

½ cup fresh flat-leaf parsley leaves

1½ tablespoons olive oil

1½ tablespoons lemon juice

½ teaspoon sumac

1 Preheat oven to 200°C/400°F. Line an oven tray with baking paper.

2 Place lentils in a large bowl; mash lightly. Add onion, garlic, pistachios, paprika, cumin, cinnamon, chilli and egg; stir to combine. Season.

3 Layer five sheets of fillo, spraying each sheet with oil (cover remaining fillo sheets with a clean, damp tea towel). Place half the lentil mixture along one long side of fillo; roll to enclose filling. Cut into four even lengths. Place on tray; spray with oil. Repeat with remaining fillo, oil spray and lentil mixture to make 8 rolls in total.

4 Sprinkle rolls with sumac; bake for 30 minutes or until golden and crisp.

5 Meanwhile, make tomato sumac salad.

6 Serve lentil rolls with salad and yoghurt.

TOMATO SUMAC SALAD Place ingredients in a large bowl; toss to combine.

WHAT'S FOR DINNER?

THAI YELLOW CURRY

PREP + COOK TIME 1 HOUR SERVES 4

1 tablespoon rice bran oil

1 medium red onion (170g), sliced thinly

¼ cup (75g) yellow curry paste

2 cloves garlic, crushed

10cm (4-inch) stick fresh lemon grass, bruised

4 fresh kaffir lime leaves, shredded finely

1⅔ cups (410ml) coconut milk

1 cup (250ml) water

750g (1½ pounds) kumara (orange sweet potato), unpeeled, scrubbed, chopped coarsely

200g (6½ ounces) green beans, trimmed

250g (8 ounces) assorted asian mushrooms

1 tablespoon finely grated palm sugar

1 tablespoon fish sauce (see Notes)

2 tablespoons lime juice

1 fresh long red chilli, seeded, sliced thinly

¼ cup (20g) fried asian shallots

½ cup fresh thai basil leaves

1 Heat oil in a wok or large saucepan over high heat; cook onion, stirring, for 5 minutes or until onion softens. Add paste, garlic, lemon grass, and kaffir lime leaves; cook, stirring, for 1 minute or until fragrant.

2 Add coconut milk, the water and kumara; bring to the boil. Reduce heat, simmer, uncovered, for 20 minutes or until kumara is just tender. Stir in beans and mushrooms; cook, uncovered, for 5 minutes or until vegetables are tender. Stir in sugar, sauce and juice; remove and discard lemon grass.

3 Serve curry sprinkled with chilli, shallots and basil.

NOTE If you are avoiding all animal derived products, use tamari instead of the fish sauce.

Test Kitchen
NOTES

Chipotle chillies are dried jalapeño chillies; they are available from some delicatessens or spice shops and markets. Substitute with 1 teaspoon smoked paprika and increase mexican chilli powder to 2 teaspoons.

CHILLI BEANS WITH CHIMICHURRI

PREP + COOK TIME 1 HOUR SERVES 4

2 chipotle chillies (see Notes)

½ cup (125ml) boiling water

1 tablespoon olive oil

1 large brown onion (200g), chopped finely

2 teaspoons ground cumin

2 teaspoons ground coriander

1 teaspoon mexican chilli powder

400g (12½ ounces) canned red kidney beans, drained, rinsed

400g (12½ ounces) canned chickpeas (garbanzo beans), drained, rinsed

2 x 400g (12½ ounces) canned diced tomatoes

¼ cup (60ml) water

½ cup fresh coriander (cilantro) sprigs

¼ cup (60g) sour cream

TORTILLA CRISPS

4 x 17cm (6¾ inch) white corn tortillas, quartered

cooking oil spray

½ teaspoon sweet paprika

CHIMICHURRI

½ small red onion (50g), chopped finely

1 clove garlic, chopped finely

½ teaspoon sweet paprika

½ cup (125ml) olive oil

1½ tablespoons red wine vinegar

½ cup finely chopped fresh flat-leaf parsley

2 tablespoons finely chopped fresh oregano

1 Place chillies in a small heatproof bowl, cover with the boiling water; stand 20 minutes. Coarsely chop chillies; discard stems. Blend or process chopped chillies with soaking liquid until smooth.

2 Meanwhile, make tortilla crisps then chimichurri.

3 Heat oil in a large saucepan over medium heat; cook onion, stirring, for 5 minutes or until onion softens. Add cumin, ground coriander and chilli powder; cook, stirring, for 1 minute or until fragrant.

4 Add beans, chickpeas, chipotle mixture, tomatoes and the water; bring to the boil. Reduce heat; cook, for 15 minutes or until sauce thickens.

5 Serve chilli beans topped with chimichurri and fresh coriander, and with tortilla crisps and sour cream.

TORTILLA CRISPS Preheat oven to 200°C/400°F. Spray tortillas with oil; sprinkle with paprika. Place on an oven tray; bake for 5 minutes or until crisp.

CHIMICHURRI Combine ingredients in a small bowl; season to taste.

SERVING SUGGESTION Serve with guacamole and lime wedges.

ZUCCHINI, BLACK BEAN & CORN ENCHILADAS

PREP + COOK TIME 1 HOUR 40 MINUTES SERVES 4

3 large zucchini (450g)

⅓ cup (80ml) olive oil

2 trimmed corn cobs (500g)

8 x 20cm (8-inch) white corn tortillas

400g (12½ ounces) canned black beans, drained, rinsed

½ cup fresh coriander (cilantro) leaves

100g (3 ounces) fetta

¼ cup fresh oregano leaves

1 tablespoon fresh oregano, extra

ENCHILADA SAUCE

800g (1½ pounds) canned crushed tomatoes

1½ cups (375ml) vegetable stock (see page 80)

2 tablespoons olive oil

2 tablespoons coarsely chopped fresh oregano

2 tablespoons apple cider vinegar

1 medium brown onion (150g), chopped coarsely

1 clove garlic, chopped

1 tablespoon chopped pickled jalapeños

1 teaspoon ground cumin

1 teaspoon caster (superfine) sugar

¼ teaspoon ground chilli powder

1 Preheat oven to 180°C/350°F. Line an oven tray with baking paper. Grease a 25cm x 30cm (10-inch x 12-inch) ovenproof dish.

2 Cut zucchini in half lengthways then cut each half into long thin wedges. Place zucchini on tray; drizzle with half the oil. Roast 30 minutes or until just tender; chop coarsely.

3 Meanwhile make enchilada sauce.

4 Brush corn with 1 tablespoon of the oil. Heat a grill plate (or grill or barbecue) over medium-high heat; cook corn, turning occasionally, for 10 minutes or until golden and tender. Using a sharp knife, cut kernels from cobs; discard cobs.

5 Reheat grill plate (or grill or barbecue) over medium-high heat; cook tortillas, for 30 seconds each side or until lightly charred. Transfer to a plate; cover to keep warm.

6 Combine zucchini, beans, coriander, half the corn, half the fetta, half the oregano and ½ cup enchilada sauce in a large bowl.

7 Divide zucchini filling evenly among warm tortillas; roll to enclose filling. Place tortillas in dish; brush tops with remaining oil. Spoon remaining enchilada sauce over tortillas, leaving 2cm (¾-inch) at each end of enchiladas uncovered. Top with remaining fetta and oregano.

8 Bake for 30 minutes or until golden and heated through. Serve topped with remaining corn and extra oregano.

ENCHILADA SAUCE Blend or process ingredients until smooth; transfer to a medium saucepan. Bring to a simmer over medium heat for 20 minutes or until thickened slightly.

ROOT VEGETABLE TRAY PIZZA

PREP + COOK TIME 1 HOUR (+ STANDING) SERVES 2

4 x 5cm (2-inch) fresh rosemary sprigs

2 cloves garlic, crushed

2 teaspoons fresh thyme leaves

⅓ cup (80ml) olive oil

4 small potatoes (480g), unpeeled, scrubbed, sliced thinly

1 small kumara (orange sweet potato) (250g), unpeeled, scrubbed, sliced thinly

1 small parsnip (120g), unpeeled, scrubbed, sliced thinly lengthways

100g (3 ounces) baby (dutch) carrots, unpeeled, scrubbed, trimmed

1 cup (115g) firmly packed trimmed watercress

2 teaspoons finely grated lemon rind

1 teaspoon lemon juice

30g (1 ounce) persian fetta, crumbled

WHOLEMEAL PIZZA DOUGH

2 teaspoons (7g) dried yeast

1 teaspoon caster (superfine) sugar

1 cup (250ml) warm water, approximately

1½ cups (225g) bread flour or plain (all-purpose) flour

1½ cups (240g) wholemeal plain (all-purpose) flour

1 teaspoon salt

¼ cup (60ml) olive oil

1 Make wholemeal pizza dough.

2 Preheat oven to 220°C/425°F. Grease a 28cm x 32cm (11¼-inch x 12¾-inch) oven tray.

3 Remove leaves from rosemary sprigs; finely chop two-thirds of the leaves. Combine chopped rosemary, garlic, thyme and 2 tablespoons of the oil in a small bowl.

4 Turn dough onto a floured surface; knead until smooth. Flatten dough; roll to a 28cm x 32cm (11¼-inch x 12¾-inch) rectangle. Carefully lift onto tray; spread rosemary mixture over base leaving a 1cm (¾-inch) border. Top with a layer of potato, kumara, parsnip and carrot; sprinkle with whole rosemary leaves. Season. Drizzle with 1 tablespoon of the oil.

5 Bake pizza for 20 minutes or until base is browned and crisp.

6 Meanwhile, combine watercress, 2 teaspoons of the oil, rind and juice in a medium bowl; season to taste.

7 Drizzle pizza with remaining oil; top with fetta and watercress salad.

WHOLEMEAL PIZZA DOUGH Combine yeast, sugar and the warm water in a small bowl; stand in a warm place for 10 minutes or until mixture is frothy. Combine flours and salt in a large bowl; stir in yeast mixture and oil, to a soft dough. Knead dough on a floured surface for 5 minutes or until smooth and elastic. Place dough in a large oiled bowl, cover; stand in a warm place for 1 hour or until dough has doubled in size.

NOTE Use a mandoline or V-slicer to slice the vegetables very thinly.

PUMPKIN & FETTA FREEFORM TART

PREP + COOK TIME 1 HOUR 30 MINUTES (+ REFRIGERATION) SERVES 4

800g (1½ pounds) jap pumpkin, cut into 3cm (1¼-inch) pieces

2 medium red onions (340g), cut into wedges

2 teaspoons fresh thyme leaves

1 tablespoon olive oil

80g (3 ounces) fetta, crumbled

2 bocconcini (70g), torn

2 tablespoons fresh thyme

CREAM CHEESE PASTRY

1¼ cups (185g) plain (all-purpose) flour

½ teaspoon sea salt flakes

125g (4 ounces) cold cream cheese, chopped

1 free-range egg

1 tablespoon cold water, approximately

MIXED LEAF SALAD

100g (3 ounces) baby mesclun

½ cup coarsely chopped fresh flat-leaf parsley

1 tablespoon fresh dill sprigs

1 medium beurre bosc pear (230g), cut into matchsticks

1 tablespoon olive oil

1 tablespoon lemon juice

1 Preheat oven to 200°C/400°F.

2 Place pumpkin, onion and thyme on a baking-paper-lined oven tray; drizzle with oil. Season. Bake for 25 minutes or until tender. Cool.

3 Meanwhile, make cream cheese pastry.

4 Roll pastry between sheets of baking paper to a 30cm (12-inch) round. Remove top sheet of baking paper; lift pastry on paper to a second oven tray. Top pastry with pumpkin mixture, fetta and bocconcini, leaving a 4cm (1½-inch) border all around. Fold pastry side over filling, pleating as you go to partially cover.

5 Bake tart for 30 minutes or until golden and base is cooked through.

6 Meanwhile, make mixed leaf salad.

7 Serve tart topped with thyme and with salad.

CREAM CHEESE PASTRY Process flour, salt and cream cheese until crumbly; add egg and the water, pulse until mixture just comes together. Knead dough on a floured surface until smooth. Wrap in plastic wrap; refrigerate for 20 minutes.

MIXED LEAF SALAD Place ingredients in a large bowl; toss gently to combine. Season to taste.

CRISP CHEESE RAVIOLI WITH SALSA VERDE

PREP + COOK TIME 45 MINUTES SERVES 6

Pan-fried ravioli is such a textural treat with a crisp exterior and molten cheese centre. We've paired it with a zingy herb sauce to cut through the richness.

130g (4 ounces) buffalo mozzarella

2 cups (200g) coarsely grated provolone cheese

36 round gow gee wrappers

5 free-range eggs, beaten lightly

3 cups (450g) panko (japanese) breadcrumbs

vegetable oil, for shallow-frying

170g (5½ ounces) asparagus, trimmed, sliced thinly lengthways (see Note)

SALSA VERDE

2 cups fresh mint leaves, chopped coarsely

2 cups fresh basil leaves, chopped coarsely

1 tablespoon drained capers, chopped finely

1 clove garlic, chopped finely

¼ cup (60ml) olive oil

¼ cup (60ml) lemon juice

2 tablespoons water

1 Drain mozzarella; pat dry with paper towel, then chop coarsely. Combine mozzarella and provolone in a medium bowl; season. Place 1 tablespoon of cheese mixture in the centre of one wrapper; brush around edges with a little water. Top with another wrapper; press edges together to seal. Repeat with remaining cheese mixture and wrappers.

2 Cook ravioli in a large saucepan of boiling water for 1 minute or until just tender; drain. Transfer to a tray lined with paper towel; set aside to cool.

3 Meanwhile, make salsa verde.

4 Carefully dip ravioli in egg, then coat in breadcrumbs. Heat 2cm (¾-inch) oil in a large deep frying pan; cook ravioli, in batches, for 1 minute each side or until golden and crisp. Drain on paper towel.

5 Serve ravioli with asparagus and the salsa verde.

SALSA VERDE Process ingredients until finely chopped; season to taste.

NOTE We used a vegetable peeler to slice the asparagus into long thin ribbons.

SEMOLINA GNOCCHI WITH MUSHROOM RAGU

PREP + COOK TIME 1 HOUR 10 MINUTES (+ REFRIGERATION) SERVES 4

20g (¾ ounce) dried porcini mushrooms

1½ cups (375ml) boiling water

3 cups (750ml) milk

50g (1½ ounces) butter, chopped coarsely

¼ cup (60ml) olive oil

1 cup (160g) fine semolina

2 free-range egg yolks

1 cup (80g) finely grated parmesan

2 shallots (50g), chopped finely

2 cloves garlic, chopped finely

250g (8 ounces) swiss brown mushrooms, sliced thickly

2 portobello mushrooms (100g), cut into wedges

2 tablespoons fresh thyme leaves

400g (12½ ounces) canned diced tomatoes

¼ cup fresh flat-leaf parsley leaves

1 Grease a 20cm x 30cm x 3cm (8-inch x 12-inch x 1¼-inch) baking pan.

2 Place porcini mushrooms in a small heatproof bowl with the boiling water; stand 10 minutes. Drain; reserve soaking liquid.

3 Bring milk, butter and 1 tablespoon of the oil to the boil in a large saucepan over high heat; gradually whisk in semolina. Reduce heat; whisk continuously for 15 minutes or until semolina thickens. Remove from heat. Add egg yolks and ¾ cup of the parmesan; stir until cheese melts. Pour mixture into pan; cool. Refrigerate for 30 minutes or until firm.

4 Meanwhile, heat remaining oil in a large frying pan over medium-high heat; cook shallots, garlic, fresh mushrooms and thyme, stirring, for 8 minutes or until tender. Add tomatoes, porcini and reserved soaking liquid; cook for 5 minutes or until thickened slightly. Season to taste.

5 Preheat grill (broiler). Line an oven tray with foil.

6 Cut semolina into 12 rectangles; place on tray, then sprinkle with remaining parmesan. Grill for 5 minutes or until golden and heated through. Serve semolina gnocchi topped with mushroom ragu and parsley.

SPINACH, CHEESE & POTATO CANNELLONI

PREP + COOK TIME 1 HOUR 35 MINUTES SERVES 6

600g (1¼ pounds) potatoes, chopped coarsely

500g (1 pound) spinach, trimmed, chopped coarsely

200g (6½ ounces) fetta, crumbled

1 cup (80g) finely grated pecorino cheese or parmesan

3 cloves garlic, chopped finely

2 tablespoons finely chopped fresh sage

¼ cup (60ml) olive oil

700g (1½ pounds) tomato passata

2 teaspoons raw sugar

400g (12½ ounces) canned diced tomatoes

¼ cup (60ml) water

250g (8 ounces) dried instant cannelloni tubes

1 Place potatoes in a large saucepan with enough cold water to just cover; bring to the boil. Boil for 15 minutes or until potato is tender; drain. Mash potato in a large bowl; season to taste.

2 Meanwhile, boil, steam or microwave spinach until wilted; drain. When cool enough to handle, squeeze excess water from spinach.

3 Add spinach to mashed potato with 150g (4½ ounces) fetta, ⅔ cup pecorino, garlic and sage; season to taste.

4 Place oil, passata, sugar, tomatoes and the water in a large saucepan over medium heat; bring to the boil. Reduce heat; simmer for 10 minutes or until reduced slightly.

5 Meanwhile, preheat oven to 180°C/350°F.

6 Using a large piping bag, fill cannelloni with potato mixture. Spread ½ cup sauce into a shallow 25cm x 32cm (10-inch x 12¾-inch) ovenproof dish; top with cannelloni, in a single layer, then top with remaining sauce, fetta and pecorino. Cover dish with foil.

7 Bake cannelloni for 30 minutes or until pasta is tender. Increase oven to 200°C/400°F, remove foil from dish; cook for a further 10 minutes or until golden.

NOTE Passata is a sieved tomato puree sold alongside other bottled pasta sauces in most supermarkets. You can use your favourite pasta sauce instead, if you prefer.

Spaghetti-like strands are created from zucchini in this recipe instead of any actual pasta, which also makes this dish a great gluten-free option.

ZUCCHINI 'SPAGHETTI' WITH TOMATO & FETTA

PREP + COOK TIME 55 MINUTES SERVES 4

500g (1 pound) cherry truss tomatoes

¼ cup (60ml) olive oil

¼ cup fresh oregano leaves

200g (6½-ounce) piece fetta, sliced into 4 lengthways

¼ teaspoon dried chilli flakes

5 small zucchini (450g)

3 cloves garlic, sliced thinly

2 teaspoons finely grated lemon rind

¼ cup (60ml) lemon juice

2 tablespoons olive oil, extra

2 tablespoons finely chopped fresh oregano, extra

1 cup small fresh basil leaves

2 tablespoons coarsely grated parmesan

1 Preheat oven to 200°C/400°F. Line two oven trays with baking paper.

2 Place tomatoes on one tray; drizzle with 1 tablespoon of the oil. Sprinkle with 2 tablespoons of the oregano leaves; season. Bake for 20 minutes or until golden and blistered.

3 Meanwhile, place fetta slices on second tray; drizzle with 1 tablespoon of the oil. Sprinkle with chilli and 2 teaspoons of the oregano. Bake for 12 minutes or until golden.

4 Using a julienne peeler or spiraliser (see Notes), cut zucchini into 'spaghetti'; place in a large bowl.

5 Heat remaining oil in a small frying pan over medium heat; cook garlic for 2 minutes or until lightly golden. Stir in rind, juice, extra oil and extra chopped oregano.

6 Add garlic mixture and roasted tomatoes (and any juices) to zucchini with basil and remaining oregano leaves; toss to combine. Season to taste. Serve 'spaghetti' topped with crumbled fetta and parmesan.

To create the long pasta-like strands, you will need a few special tools: a julienne peeler, this looks like a wide bladed vegetable peeler with a serrated rather than straight blade. You could also use a spiraliser, a hand cranked machine designed to cut vegetables into noodles or ribbons. Both items are available from kitchenware shops.

MUSHROOM, SAGE & BUCKWHEAT RISOTTO

PREP + COOK TIME 1 HOUR SERVES 4

¼ cup (60ml) olive oil

200g (6½ ounces) button mushrooms, sliced thinly

450g (14½ ounces) flat mushrooms, sliced thinly

1 medium onion (150g), chopped finely

3 cloves garlic, sliced thinly

2 tablespoons chopped fresh sage leaves

1½ cups (300g) buckwheat

1 cup (250ml) dry white wine

1.25 litres (5 cups) vegetable stock (see page 80), warmed

1 cup (80g) finely grated parmesan

2 tablespoons olive oil, extra

⅓ cup fresh sage leaves, extra

200g (6½ ounces) labne (see Note)

⅓ cup (55g) toasted flaked almonds

1 Heat 2 tablespoons of the oil in a large saucepan over high heat; cook mushrooms, in two batches, for 10 minutes or until golden. Remove from pan.

2 Reheat remaining oil in same pan over medium heat; cook onion, garlic and chopped sage for 5 minutes or until onion softens. Add buckwheat; cook, stirring, for 1 minute or until coated. Add wine; cook, stirring, for 1 minute.

3 Add stock; bring to the boil. Reduce heat to low; simmer, uncovered, for 30 minutes, stirring occasionally or until buckwheat is tender. Stir in mushrooms and parmesan; season to taste

4 Meanwhile, heat extra oil in a small frying pan over medium heat; cook extra sage for 30 seconds or until crisp. Drain on paper towel.

5 Serve risotto topped with labne, crisp sage and almonds.

NOTE Buckwheat is available from health food stores. Labne is a soft fresh cheese made from strained yoghurt, generally it is rolled into balls and stored in olive oil. You can use soft goat's cheese if unavailable.

LEBANESE ROASTED PUMPKIN SALAD

PREP + COOK TIME 1 HOUR 15 MINUTES SERVES 6

2 tablespoons honey

1 cup (100g) walnuts

2kg (4 pounds) jap pumpkin, cut into 2.5cm (1-inch) thick wedges

1 large red capsicum (bell pepper) (350g), sliced thickly

1 large red onion (300g), cut into wedges

2 tablespoons olive oil

400g (12½ ounces) canned lentils, drained, rinsed

60g (2 ounces) watercress

LEBANESE SPICE MIX

1 teaspoon sweet paprika

1 teaspoon ground cumin

1 teaspoon ground coriander

1 teaspoon ground cardamom

½ teaspoon ground cinnamon

½ teaspoon ground nutmeg

YOGHURT DRESSING

½ cup (140g) greek-style yoghurt

¼ cup (60ml) olive oil

1 tablespoon finely grated lemon rind

¼ cup (60ml) lemon juice

1 tablespoon honey

1 Preheat oven to 200°C/400°F. Line three oven trays with baking paper.

2 Make lebanese spice mix.

3 Bring honey to the boil in a small frypan over medium heat. Add walnuts and 1 teaspoon spice mix; toss gently to coat. Transfer to a tray; set aside to cool.

4 Place pumpkin on a tray and capsicum and onion on remaining tray. Drizzle with 2 tablespoons oil and remaining spice mix; toss to coat. Bake for 30 minutes or until capsicum and onion are tender; remove from oven.

5 Meanwhile, make yoghurt dressing.

6 Serve roasted vegetables with lentils, watercress, nuts and yoghurt dressing.

LEBANESE SPICE MIX Combine ingredients in a small bowl.

YOGHURT DRESSING Combine ingredients in a small bowl; season to taste.

Test Kitchen **NOTES**

Make extra spice mix and store in an airtight container for up to 1 month.

Test Kitchen NOTES

Inca berries are dried physalis peruviana or, as they are also known, cape gooseberries. The dried fruit is marketed under various names: Pichuberry in America and goldenberry in England. The fresh orange fruit, which is the size of a cherry tomato, is contained in a green paper-like calyx. The dried fruit has a tangy citrus-like taste, is high in protein (for a fruit), fibre and high in antioxidants. If you can't find them, use dried cranberries instead or 1 medium orange, peeled and segmented.

CAULIFLOWER 'COUSCOUS' WITH ROASTED CARROT HUMMUS

PREP + COOK TIME 45 MINUTES SERVES 4

900g (1¾ pounds) cauliflower, trimmed, chopped coarsely

1 tablespoon olive oil

2 tablespoons ground cumin

½ teaspoon ground cardamom

⅓ cup (45g) coarsely chopped, roasted unsalted pistachios

⅓ cup (50g) roasted pine nuts

½ cup (100g) pomegranate seeds

1 cup fresh flat-leaf parsley leaves, chopped coarsely

1 cup fresh mint leaves, chopped coarsely

½ cup (60g) inca berries (see Notes)

1 tablespoon finely chopped preserved lemon rind

1 medium lemon (140g), cut into wedges

ROASTED CARROT HUMMUS

3 medium carrots (360g), chopped coarsely

2 teaspoons olive oil

300g (9½ ounces) hummus

1 teaspoon finely grated orange rind

1 Make roasted carrot hummus.

2 Meanwhile, process cauliflower until it resembles couscous. Heat oil in a large frying pan or wok over medium heat; cook cauliflower, stirring, for 5 minutes or until tender. Add cumin and cardamom; cook for 1 minute or until fragrant, season to taste.

3 Combine cauliflower mixture, nuts, seeds, parsley, mint, berries and preserved lemon in a large bowl. Serve topped with hummus and lemon wedges.

ROASTED CARROT HUMMUS Preheat oven to 180°C/350°F. Place carrots on a baking-paper-lined oven tray; drizzle with oil. Roast for 40 minutes or until tender; cool slightly. Blend or process carrots with remaining ingredients until smooth and combined. Season to taste.

SMOKED TOFU SALAD WITH PEANUT DRESSING

PREP + COOK TIME 45 MINUTES SERVES 4

4 free-range eggs

¼ cup (60ml) water

1 tablespoon fried asian shallots

1 teaspoon tamari

1 tablespoon sesame oil

350g (11 ounces) smoked tofu, cut into 1cm (½-inch) pieces (see Notes)

1 medium avocado (250g), sliced thinly

250g (8 ounces) cherry tomatoes, halved

1½ cup (120g) bean sprouts

½ cup fresh coriander (cilantro) leaves

½ cup fresh vietnamese mint leaves

75g (2½ ounces) baby salad leaves

2 tablespoons black sesame seeds

PEANUT DRESSING

⅓ cup (45g) roasted peanuts, chopped coarsely

1 green onion (scallion), sliced thinly

1 fresh long red chilli, sliced thinly

1 teaspoon finely grated fresh ginger

1 clove garlic, crushed

1½ tablespoons grated palm sugar

2 tablespoons sesame oil

2 tablespoons tamari

¼ cup (60ml) rice vinegar

1½ tablespoons lime juice

1 Make peanut dressing.

2 Whisk eggs, the water, shallots and tamari in a large bowl; season.

3 Heat oil in a wok over medium heat. Pour half the egg mixture into wok; cook, tilting wok, until almost set. Remove omelette from wok. Repeat with remaining egg mixture. Roll omelettes tightly, then slice thinly; reserve.

4 Place tofu in a large bowl with remaining ingredients and the peanut dressing; toss to combine.

5 Serve tofu salad topped with the reserved omelette.

PEANUT DRESSING Whisk ingredients in a medium bowl until combined.

Test Kitchen
NOTES

Smoked tofu can be found at health food stores, you can however use regular hard tofu instead for this recipe.

Vietnamese mint can be found in Asian supermarkets.

To keep bean sprouts crisp and crunchy, store them in cold water in the fridge for up to 3 days.

Test Kitchen NOTES

Use the freshest, best radishes you can buy. The radishes should be firm, and the leaves crisp and bright green. We used 16 radishes and about 2½ cups of radish leaves in this recipe.

PASTA WITH RADISHES & THEIR TOPS

PREP + COOK TIME 20 MINUTES SERVES 4

This dish which utilises both the radish bulbs and tops, embodies the sustainability concept of root to leaf eating, where nothing goes to waste.

¼ cup (40g) currants

1½ tablespoons red wine vinegar

1kg (2 pounds) baby red radishes, halved, leaves reserved (see Notes)

375g (12 ounces) dried spelt or wholemeal penne pasta

⅓ cup (80ml) extra virgin olive oil

1 clove garlic, crushed

⅓ cup (50g) toasted pine nuts

¼ cup fresh sage leaves

½ cup (40g) shaved pecorino cheese

1 Combine currants and vinegar in a small bowl; stand for 15 minutes.
2 Meanwhile, coarsely chop reserved radish leaves.
3 Cook pasta in a large saucepan of boiling salted water until almost tender. Drain, reserving 1 cup cooking liquid.
4 Meanwhile, heat oil in a large frying pan over high heat; cook radishes, stirring occasionally, for 3 minutes or until browned. Add currant mixture, radish leaves, garlic, pine nuts and sage; cook, stirring, for 1 minute or until fragrant and leaves are wilted. Season.
5 Add pasta to the frying pan with half the cheese, the remaining oil and enough of the reserved cooking liquid to coat; season to taste. Serve topped with remaining cheese.

SILVER BEET OMELETTE WITH CAPSICUM SALAD

PREP + COOK TIME 35 MINUTES SERVES 4

260g (8½ ounces) chargrilled red capsicum (bell pepper), drained, sliced thickly

1 tablespoon fresh thyme leaves

1 clove garlic, crushed

1 tablespoon balsamic vinegar

1 tablespoon olive oil

6 medium stalks silver beet (swiss chard)

10 free-range eggs

¼ cup (60ml) milk

2 cloves garlic, extra, crushed

3 cups (350g) firmly packed snow pea tendrils

½ cup (40g) shaved pecorino cheese

1 Combine capsicum, thyme, garlic, vinegar and oil in a large bowl; stand for 15 minutes.
2 Meanwhile, cut stems from silver beet (save for another use if you like); shred leaves. Whisk eggs, milk, shredded silver beet and extra garlic in a large bowl; season.
3 Heat a small non-stick frying pan over medium heat. Pour one-quarter of the egg mixture into pan; tilt pan to cover base with egg mixture. Cook over medium heat for 3 minutes or until omelette is just set. Carefully slide omelette onto plate; cover to keep warm. Repeat with remaining egg mixture to make 4 omelettes in total.
4 Add snow pea tendrils and pecorino to capsicum mixture; toss to combine.
5 Serve omelettes topped with capsicum salad.

SEE PHOTO PAGE 64

Silver beet omelette
with capsicum salad
(recipe on page 63)

Test Kitchen NOTES

Nigella seeds, also known as kolonji, are the seeds sprinkled on Turkish bread. They are available from delis and greengrocers that stock spices, otherwise substitute cumin seeds.

Before using tahini always stir the oil that sits on top of the paste back into it and ensure that any liquid that is added to thin tahini is cold and not hot, otherwise it will have the opposite effect and thicken the tahini.

Roasted cauliflower & brussels sprouts (recipe on page 66)

ROASTED CAULIFLOWER & BRUSSELS SPROUTS

PREP + COOK TIME 45 MINUTES SERVES 4

⅓ cup (80ml) olive oil

1½ teaspoons ground cumin

1 teaspoon nigella seeds (see Notes page 65)

2 teaspoons toasted sesame seeds

2 tablespoons honey

1 small cauliflower (1kg), trimmed, cut into florets

500g (1 pound) brussels sprouts, cut in half

¼ cup (40g) pine nuts

2 tablespoons fresh coriander (cilantro) leaves

2 tablespoons fresh mint leaves

TAHINI DRESSING

½ cup (90g) tahini

⅓ cup (80ml) lemon juice

1 clove garlic, crushed

¼ cup (60ml) cold water

2 tablespoons finely chopped fresh coriander (cilantro)

2 tablespoons finely chopped fresh mint

1 Preheat oven to 220°C/425°F. Line an oven tray with baking paper.
2 Combine oil, cumin, seeds and honey in a large bowl; season. Add cauliflower and sprouts; toss to combine. Place vegetable mixture on tray.
3 Bake for 15 minutes or until vegetables are almost tender. Add nuts to tray; bake for a further 5 minutes or until nuts are golden and vegetables are tender.
4 Meanwhile, make tahini dressing.
5 Serve vegetables topped with herbs and drizzled with tahini dressing.

TAHINI DRESSING Combine ingredients in a small bowl; season to taste.

MISO BROTH WITH TAMARI PUMPKIN & NOODLES

PREP + COOK TIME 55 MINUTES SERVES 4

⅓ cup (80g) red miso paste

¼ cup (60ml) tamari

1 tablespoon olive oil

600g (1¼ pounds) butternut pumpkin, cut into 2.5cm (1-inch) thick wedges

1.5 litres (6 cups) water

40g (1½-ounce) piece fresh ginger, cut into matchsticks

140g (4½ ounces) dried soba noodles

250g (8 ounces) gai lan (chinese broccoli), trimmed

¼ cup shredded dried seaweed (nori)

2 green onions (scallions), sliced thinly

2 tablespoons toasted sesame seeds

1 Preheat oven to 200°C/400°F. Line an oven tray with baking paper.
2 Whisk 1 tablespoon miso, 2 tablespoons tamari and oil in a large bowl. Add pumpkin; toss to coat. Place pumpkin, in a single layer, on tray. Roast for 40 minutes or until golden and tender.
3 Meanwhile, bring the water, ginger and remaining miso to the boil in a large saucepan. Add noodles and gai lan; return to the boil. Reduce heat; simmer, for 2 minutes or until noodles are tender. Stir in remaining tamari; season to taste.
4 Divide pumpkin and broth into bowls; sprinkle with seaweed, green onion and seeds. Serve with warm flatbread, if you like.

Just before serving, you could sprinkle this dish with a little shichimi tōgarashi – a Japanese spice powder (literally meaning "seven flavour chilli pepper"). In addition to the chillies, other ingredients can include: sichuan pepper, dried citrus peel, sesame seeds, poppy seeds, hemp seeds, ginger, garlic, shiso, and nori. It is readily available from Asian supermarkets. If unavailable you can use dried chilli flakes.

SRI LANKAN POTATO & PEA CURRY

PREP + COOK TIME 45 MINUTES SERVES 4

4 medium potatoes (800g), chopped coarsely

¼ cup (60g) ghee (clarified butter)

1 medium brown onion (150g), sliced thinly

4 cloves garlic, chopped finely

2½ tablespoons finely chopped fresh ginger

2 sprigs fresh curry leaves

1 tablespoon curry powder

1½ teaspoons brown mustard seeds

½ teaspoon ground turmeric

2 fresh long green chillies, sliced thinly

400g (12½ ounces) canned chickpeas (garbanzo beans), drained, rinsed

1 cup (120g) frozen peas

½ cup (125ml) water

½ teaspoon finely grated lime rind

1 tablespoon lime juice

4 free-range eggs

2 green onions (scallions), sliced thinly

1 cup fresh coriander (cilantro) leaves

1 Place potatoes in a large saucepan with enough cold water to just cover; bring to the boil. Boil over medium heat for 15 minutes or until tender; drain.

2 Heat 2 tablespoons of the ghee in a large frying pan over medium heat; cook onion, stirring, for 5 minutes or until softened. Add garlic, ginger, curry leaves, curry powder, seeds, turmeric and half the chilli; cook, stirring, for 1 minute or until fragrant.

3 Add potatoes, chickpeas, peas and the water; bring to the boil. Reduce heat; simmer, for 3 minutes or until peas are tender. Stir in rind and juice; season to taste.

4 Heat remaining ghee in a large frying pan over medium-high heat; fry eggs for 2 minutes or until the whites are set.

5 Serve potato curry topped with fried egg, green onions, coriander and remaining chilli.

NOTE We used dutch cream potatoes.

TOMATO, TOFU & CHILLI PILAF

PREP + COOK TIME 35 MINUTES SERVES 6

60g (2 ounces) butter

2 small red onions (200g), sliced thinly

200g (11 ounces) thai-flavoured marinated tofu, cut into 2.5cm (1-inch) pieces (see Note)

1½ cups (300g) jasmine rice

1 fresh long red chilli, seeded, chopped finely

2 tablespoons thai red curry paste

2 teaspoons finely grated ginger

400g (12½ ounces) canned chopped tomatoes

1½ cups (375ml) boiling water

100g (3 ounces) snow peas, trimmed

¼ cup (35g) roasted peanuts, chopped coarsely

2 green onions (scallions), sliced thinly

¼ cup fresh coriander (cilantro) sprigs

1 lime (65g), cut into wedges

1 Heat butter in a 26cm (10½-inch) frying pan over medium heat; cook red onion and tofu, stirring occasionally, for 5 minutes or until onion softens and tofu browns slightly.

2 Meanwhile, place rice in a sieve; rinse under cold running water until water runs clear. Set aside.

3 Add chilli, curry paste and ginger to pan; increase heat to high. Stir for 3 minutes or until mixture starts to stick a little and caramelise. Stir in rinsed rice until well coated. Add tomatoes and the water; season generously with salt.

4 Bring to the boil, cover with a lid; reduce heat to low, cook for 15 minutes or until liquid is absorbed. Remove pan from heat; place snow peas on rice. Cover pan; stand, for 5 minutes (the residual heat will finish cooking the snow peas and rice).

5 Serve pilaf topped with peanuts, green onions, coriander and lime wedges.

NOTE We used SoyCo marinated tofu available from supermarkets. You could use another flavoured tofu or even plain tofu instead, if you prefer.

GREEN GOODNESS IN A BOWL

PREP + COOK TIME 20 MINUTES SERVES 4

150g (4½ ounces) snow peas, trimmed

200g (6½ ounces) green beans, trimmed, halved lengthways

200g (6½ ounces) broccolini, halved on the diagonal

2 teaspoons olive oil

500g (1 pound) packaged brown microwave rice

2 tablespoons pepitas (pumpkin seeds), toasted, chopped coarsely

1 medium avocado (250g), sliced thinly

1 tablespoon pepitas (pumpkin seeds), toasted, extra

AVOCADO YOGHURT DRESSING

1 medium avocado (250g), chopped coarsely

¾ cup (200g) greek-style yoghurt

¼ cup fresh basil leaves

2 tablespoons lime juice

1 small clove garlic, chopped finely

1 tablespoon olive oil

1 tablespoon water

1 Make avocado yoghurt dressing.

2 Boil, steam or microwave peas, beans and broccolini, separately, until tender; drain. Place peas, beans and broccolini in a large bowl with oil; toss to combine. Cover to keep warm.

3 Cook rice following instructions on packet. Combine rice and chopped pepitas in a medium bowl; season to taste.

4 Serve rice topped with three-quarters of the dressing, then vegetables, avocado, remaining dressing and extra pepitas.

AVOCADO YOGHURT DRESSING Blend or process ingredients until smooth and combined; season to taste.

Test Kitchen NOTES

For a spicy version, add 2 teaspoons chopped pickled jalapeños to the dressing.

ROAST VEGETABLES WITH BASIL & FETTA POLENTA

PREP + COOK TIME 50 MINUTES SERVES 6

500g (1 pound) pumpkin, chopped coarsely

2 large zucchini (300g), chopped coarsely

2 medium red onions (340g), quartered

2 large red capsicums (bell peppers) (700g), chopped coarsely

1 tablespoon cumin seeds

2 teaspoons ground coriander

½ teaspoon dried chilli flakes

2 cloves garlic, crushed

¼ cup (60ml) olive oil

2 tablespoons red wine vinegar

1.5 litres (6 cups) vegetable stock (see page 80)

1½ cups (250g) polenta (cornmeal)

200g (6½ ounces) danish fetta, crumbled

½ cup torn fresh basil

⅓ cup (45g) coarsely chopped toasted hazelnuts

1 Preheat oven to 220°C/425°F. Line two large oven trays with baking paper.

2 Combine pumpkin, zucchini, onion, capsicum, cumin, coriander, chilli, garlic and oil in a large bowl; season. Place vegetables on trays; roast for 30 minutes or until golden and tender. Drizzle with vinegar.

3 Meanwhile, bring stock to the boil in a large saucepan. Gradually add polenta, whisking continuously. Reduce heat; simmer, stirring, for 10 minutes or until polenta thickens. Stir in 125g (4 ounces) of the fetta and ⅓ cup of the basil.

4 Serve polenta immediately, topped with vegetables, hazelnuts, remaining fetta and remaining basil.

Harissa is a hot chilli paste; there are many different brands available on the market, and the strengths vary enormously. Harissa in a tube is generally much hotter than brands from a jar. Taste a little first before using.

CHICKPEA SHAKSHUKA

PREP + COOK TIME 30 MINUTES SERVES 4

1 teaspoon caraway seeds

1 teaspoon cumin seeds

1 teaspoon smoked paprika

2 tablespoons olive oil

2 cloves garlic, crushed

1 fresh long red chilli, chopped finely

1 large brown onion (200g), chopped coarsely

1 large red capsicum (bell pepper) (350g), chopped coarsely

400g (12½ ounces) canned chickpeas (garbanzo beans), drained, rinsed

400g (12½ ounces) canned diced tomatoes

1 cup (250ml) water

2 teaspoons harissa (see Notes)

2 teaspoons caster (superfine) sugar

4 free-range eggs

¼ cup fresh coriander (cilantro) leaves

1 Heat a large, deep ovenproof frying pan over a medium heat; cook seeds and paprika, stirring, for 1 minute or until fragrant. Add oil, garlic and chilli; cook for 1 minute or until fragrant.

2 Add onion and capsicum; cook, stirring, for 8 minutes or until onion is softened. Add chickpeas, tomatoes, the water, harrisa and sugar; bring to the boil. Reduce heat; simmer, for 5 minutes or until vegetables are tender and liquid has thickened slightly.

3 Using a spoon, make four shallow indents in the tomato mixture. Crack 1 egg into each hole. Cook, covered, on low heat, for 5 minutes or until whites are set and yolks still remain runny, or until cooked to your liking. Serve topped with coriander.

SERVING SUGGESTION Serve with baked chia seed mountain bread wraps and chilli oil. Preheat oven to 220°C/425°F. Spray wraps with cooking oil; cut wraps into quarters. Bake for 8 minutes or until golden and crisp.

POTATO, CAPSICUM & SPINACH FRITTATA

PREP + COOK TIME 40 MINUTES SERVES 4

500g (1 pound) baby new potatoes

8 free-range eggs

⅔ cup (160ml) milk

1 tablespoon olive oil

100g (3 ounces) baby spinach leaves

1 cup (240g) chargrilled red capsicum (bell pepper), drained, chopped coarsely

100g (3 ounces) soft goat's cheese, crumbled

1 tablespoon lemon rind strips (see Notes)

OLIVE SALSA

¼ cup (55g) pitted kalamata olives, chopped

¼ cup (40g) pitted green sicilian olives, chopped

¼ cup (40g) pitted green olives, chopped

½ small red onion (50g), chopped finely

¼ cup chopped fresh flat-leaf parsley

pinch dried chilli flakes

1 tablespoon olive oil

2 teaspoons lemon juice

1 Place potatoes in a medium saucepan with enough cold water to just cover. Boil over medium heat for 15 minutes or until potato is tender; drain. Cut into 2.5cm (1-inch) pieces.

2 Meanwhile, make olive salsa.

3 Whisk eggs and milk in a medium bowl; season.

4 Preheat grill (broiler).

5 Heat oil in a heavy-based frying pan over medium-high heat; cook spinach until wilted. Add potatoes and capsicum; cook, stirring, for 1 minute. Add egg mixture. Reduce heat to medium; cook for 7 minutes or until egg is almost set. Top with cheese. Place under heated grill for 3 minutes or until golden and set.

6 Serve frittata with salsa; sprinkle with lemon rind.

OLIVE SALSA Combine ingredients in a small bowl.

If you have one, use a zester to create the strips of lemon rind. If you don't have one, peel two long, wide strips of rind from the lemon, without the white pith, then cut them lengthways into thin strips.

STOCKS

VEGETABLE STOCK

PREP + COOK TIME 2 HOURS 30 MINUTES MAKES 2.5 LITRES (10 CUPS)

Stock is simple to prepare and will boost the flavour of any dish. The key to preparing flavoursome stocks is a gentle simmer. If you boil the stock you will not create a well-developed flavour.

Coarsely chop 1 medium (350g) leek, 1 large (200g) unpeeled brown onion, 2 large (360g) carrots, 1 large (400g) swede, 2 celery stalks (with leaves) (300g) and 3 unpeeled garlic cloves. Place vegetables in a boiler with 1 teaspoon black peppercorns, 1 bouquet garni (see Notes opposite) and 5 litres (20 cups) water; bring to the boil. Reduce heat; simmer, uncovered, for 2 hours. Strain stock through a sieve into a large heatproof bowl; discard solids. Allow stock to cool. Cover; refrigerate until cold.

Test Kitchen
NOTES

For a bouquet garni, tie 3 fresh bay leaves, 2 sprigs fresh rosemary, 6 sprigs fresh thyme and 6 fresh flat-leaf parsley stalks together with kitchen string.

Keep vegetable peelings from meal preparations in a bowl in the fridge to add to stock. This is sustainable and adds flavour

Freeze any leftover stock in ice cube trays for later use.

ITALIAN-STYLE STOCK

Coarsely chop 2 large (400g) unpeeled brown onions, 2 large (360g) carrots, 2 celery stalks (with leaves) (300g) and 3 unpeeled cloves garlic. Place ingredients in a boiler with 1 teaspoon black peppercorns, 1 bouquet garni (see Notes page 81), 1 parmesan rind, 1 teaspoon fennel seeds, 400g (12½ ounces) canned whole peeled tomatoes and 5 litres (20 cups) water. Cook following the directions for vegetable stock (page 80).

ASIAN-STYLE STOCK

Coarsely chop 1 medium (350g) leek, 2 large (360g) carrots, 2 celery stalks (with leaves) (300g), 3 unpeeled cloves garlic, 10cm (4-inch) piece fresh ginger and 4 green onions (scallions). Place ingredients in a boiler with 1 teaspoon black peppercorns, 20 sprigs fresh coriander (cilantro), 1 cinnamon stick, 3 whole star anise, ½ cup (125ml) tamari and 5 litres (20 cups) water. Cook following the directions for vegetable stock (page 80).

VEGAN

EGGPLANT MA PO TOFU

PREP + COOK TIME 35 MINUTES SERVES 4

6 baby (finger) eggplants (360g),
halved lengthways, scored

2 tablespoons vegetable oil

2 cloves garlic, sliced thinly

20g (¾-ounce) piece fresh ginger,
cut into matchsticks

4 green onions (scallions), sliced thinly

3 shiitake mushrooms (45g), sliced thinly

1½ tablespoons chilli bean sauce

½ cup (125ml) vegetable stock (see page 80)

1 tablespoon soy sauce

600g (1¼ pounds) silken tofu,
cut into 5cm (2-inch) pieces

1 teaspoon cornflour (cornstarch)

2 tablespoons water

2 teaspoons toasted sichuan pepper, ground

2 tablespoons coarsely chopped fresh
garlic chives

1 Steam eggplant, covered, over a large
wok of simmering water for 20 minutes
or until tender.
2 Meanwhile, heat oil in a large wok over high
heat; stir-fry garlic, ginger and half the green
onion for 30 seconds or until fragrant. Add
mushrooms and chilli bean sauce; stir-fry for
1 minute. Add stock and soy sauce; bring to
the boil. Add tofu; reduce heat, simmer, for
3 minutes or until warmed through.
3 Combine cornflour with the water in a small
bowl; add to tofu mixture. Return to the boil;
boil until mixture thickens. Remove from heat.
Stir in ground pepper and three-quarters of
the chives.
4 Serve eggplant topped with tofu mixture,
sprinkled with remaining chives and
remaining green onion.

GREEN DUMPLINGS WITH SOY CHILLI DIPPING SAUCE

PREP + COOK TIME 45 MINUTES SERVES 4 AS A LIGHT MEAL

300g (9½ ounces) spinach, trimmed

125g (4 ounces) gai lan
(chinese broccoli) leaves

1 cup fresh finely chopped garlic chives

2 tablespoons soy sauce

2 cloves garlic, grated finely

1½ tablespoons finely grated fresh ginger

2 teaspoons sesame oil

240g (7½ ounces) round gow gee wrappers

SOY CHILLI DIPPING SAUCE

¼ cup (60ml) soy sauce

2 tablespoons chinese black vinegar

1 teaspoon caster (superfine) sugar

1 teaspoon sesame oil

1 teaspoon chilli oil

1 green onion (scallion), sliced thinly

1 Boil, steam or microwave spinach and gai lan until tender; drain. Rinse under cold water; drain. Squeeze out excess water; chop finely.
2 Combine spinach, gai lan, chives, sauce, garlic, ginger and oil in a medium bowl.
3 Place 2 teaspoons of mixture in the centre of a gow gee wrapper. Wet edge of wrapper with fingers; fold in half and press edges together to seal. Repeat with remaining wrappers and mixture.
4 Cook dumplings, in batches, in a large saucepan of boiling water, for 2 minutes, or until they float and are just tender. Drain.
5 Meanwhile, make soy chilli dipping sauce.
6 Serve dumplings with dipping sauce.

SOY CHILLI DIPPING SAUCE Combine ingredients in a small bowl.

NOTE To turn this recipe into a dumpling soup, serve dumplings in vegetable stock (see page 80).

Test Kitchen NOTES

We used a julienne peeler to easily cut the carrot into long thin strips. They are available from kitchenware shops and most major supermarkets.

VIETNAMESE COCONUT & TURMERIC PANCAKES

PREP + COOK TIME 25 MINUTES (+ STANDING) SERVES 4

⅔ cup (160ml) coconut milk

⅔ cup (160ml) water

½ cup (90g) rice flour

1 teaspoon ground turmeric

¼ cup (60ml) vegetable oil

300g (9½ ounces) tempeh, cut into 8 slices

2 tablespoons hoisin sauce

8 butter (boston) lettuce leaves

2 lebanese cucumbers (260g), cut into matchsticks

1 cup fresh vietnamese mint leaves

1 cup fresh coriander (cilantro) leaves

1 cup fresh thai basil leaves

1 cup (80g) bean sprouts

PICKLED CARROT

⅓ cup (80ml) rice wine vinegar

2 teaspoons caster (superfine) sugar

2 medium carrots (240g), cut into matchsticks (see Notes)

1 fresh long red chilli, sliced thinly

LEMON GARLIC DIPPING SAUCE

¼ cup (60ml) lemon juice

2 teaspoons caster (superfine) sugar

2 teaspoons soy sauce

1 small clove garlic, chopped finely

1 Whisk coconut milk, the water, flour and turmeric in a medium bowl until smooth and combined. Stand for 1 hour.

2 Meanwhile, make pickled carrot, then lemon garlic dipping sauce.

3 Heat 1 tablespoon oil in a large, non-stick frying pan over medium high heat; cook tempeh for 1 minute or until golden. Remove from pan.

4 Heat 2 teaspoons oil in a large non-stick frying pan over medium-high heat. Pour one-quarter of the batter into pan, tilt pan to cover base with batter; cook for 2 minutes or until pancake is just set. Carefully slide pancake onto plate; cover with foil to keep warm. Repeat with remaining batter to make 4 pancakes in total.

5 Spread pancakes with hoisin sauce; top with tempeh, lettuce, cucumber, pickled carrot, herbs and sprouts. Serve with dipping sauce.

PICKLED CARROT Whisk vinegar and sugar in a large bowl; add carrot and chilli, then toss to combine. Stand, stirring occasionally, for 15 minutes.

LEMON GARLIC DIPPING SAUCE Whisk ingredients in a small bowl; season to taste.

Test Kitchen NOTES

Harissa is a hot chilli paste; there are many different brands available on the market, and the strengths vary enormously. Harissa in a tube is generally much hotter than brands from a jar. Taste a little first before using.

In ancient times millet was more widely consumed in Asia than rice is today. Like rice it is gluten free, making it suitable for those on low, or gluten-free diets. It is almost always sold in its wholegrain form in health food stores and so provides fibre, B group vitamins and plant proteins.

ROASTED BEETROOT & MILLET SALAD

PREP + COOK TIME 1 HOUR 20 MINUTES SERVES 4

1kg (2 pounds) baby beetroots (beets), unpeeled, trimmed

¼ cup (60ml) olive oil

⅔ cup (130g) hulled millet (see Notes)

2 cups (500ml) water

1 medium fennel (300g), sliced thinly

½ small red onion (50g), sliced thinly

6 stalks rainbow chard, shredded finely

⅓ cup (45g) coarsely chopped, roasted unsalted pistachios

2 tablespoons coarsely chopped fresh dill

¼ cup coarsely chopped fresh flat-leaf parsley

HARISSA DRESSING

¼ cup (60ml) olive oil

1½ tablespoons sherry vinegar

3 teaspoons harissa (see Notes)

1 tablespoon lemon juice

1 Preheat oven to 200°C/400°F. Line an oven tray with baking paper.

2 Place beetroot on tray; drizzle with oil. Roast for 50 minutes or until tender. Peel and discard skins; halve or quarter beetroot depending on size.

3 Meanwhile, place millet in a medium saucepan, cover with water; bring to the boil, stirring occasionally. Reduce heat; simmer, for 15 minutes or until millet is almost tender. Drain. Return millet to pan with remaining oil; cook, stirring, over medium heat for 3 minutes or until millet is dry. Season to taste.

4 Meanwhile, make harissa dressing.

5 Place beetroot and millet in a large bowl with fennel, onion, chard, pistachio, herbs and dressing; toss gently to combine.

HARISSA DRESSING Place ingredients in a screw-top jar; shake well. Season to taste.

BROCCOLINI & ASPARAGUS WITH VEGAN YOGHURT

PREP + COOK TIME 25 MINUTES SERVES 2

½ cup (80g) whole blanched almonds

1 teaspoon olive oil

1 teaspoon sweet paprika

200g (6½ ounces) broccolini, trimmed

340g (11 ounces) asparagus, trimmed

40g (1½ ounces) baby beetroot (beet) leaves (see Notes)

½ cup fresh mint leaves

½ cup (110g) vegan yoghurt (see page 106)

CHILLI GARLIC DRESSING

¼ cup (60ml) olive oil

1 fresh long red chilli, seeded, sliced thinly

2 cloves garlic, sliced thinly

1 teaspoon finely chopped fresh ginger

1 teaspoon coriander seeds, crushed

2 tablespoons red wine vinegar

1 Preheat oven to 180°C/350°F. Line an oven tray with baking paper.

2 Place almonds on tray; drizzle with a little of the oil and sprinkle with paprika. Toss to combine; season. Bake for 8 minutes or until golden; set aside to cool. Chop coarsely.

3 Meanwhile, make chilli garlic dressing.

4 Boil, steam or microwave broccolini and asparagus until tender; drain. Rinse under cold water; drain.

5 Serve broccolini and asparagus with beetroot leaves, mint and chopped almonds; drizzle with dressing and dollop with yoghurt.

CHILLI GARLIC DRESSING Heat oil in a small frypan over low heat; cook chilli, garlic, ginger and seeds, stirring, 1 minute or until fragrant. Remove from heat; stir in vinegar.

You will need 1 bunch of broccolini and 2 bunches of asparagus for this recipe. Baby beet leaves are available from specialist green grocers and growers' markets. You can substitute with baby spinach leaves.

You can prepare batches of paprika almonds and store them in an airtight container for up to 2 weeks. Add almonds to salads or eat them as a snack.

KUMARA & 'CHORIZO' TACOS

PREP + COOK TIME 40 MINUTES SERVES 4

2 small kumara (orange sweet potato) (500g), unpeeled

½ cup (125ml) olive oil

6 green onions (scallions), chopped coarsely

1 teaspoon ground cumin

1 teaspoon ground coriander

2 cups coarsely chopped fresh coriander (cilantro) roots and stems

2 fresh jalapeño chillies, chopped coarsely

1½ teaspoons finely grated lime rind

2 tablespoons lime juice

⅓ cup (80ml) water

500g (1 pound) bottled sun-dried tomatoes in oil

¼ teaspoon garlic powder

¼ teaspoon onion powder

½ teaspoon smoked paprika

¼ cup (40g) roasted whole blanched almonds

¼ cup (25g) roasted walnuts

12 x 17cm (6¾-inch) white corn tortillas, warmed

40g (1½ ounces) baby rocket (arugula) leaves

1 Boil, steam or microwave kumara until tender; drain. When cool enough to handle, peel kumara; cut flesh into 1.5cm (¾-inch) pieces.

2 Meanwhile, blend or process oil, onion, cumin, ground and fresh coriander, chillies, rind, juice and the water in a food processor until smooth. Transfer to a small bowl; stand until required.

3 Drain oil from tomatoes over a bowl; reserve. Coarsely chop tomatoes. Process tomatoes and 2 tablespoons of the reserved oil with garlic and onion powders, paprika and nuts until coarsely chopped. Add 2 tablespoons of coriander mixture; pulse until combined.

4 Transfer tomato mixture to a large frying pan, stir in kumara. Heat mixture over low heat for 5 minutes or until warmed through. Serve kumara mixture in tortillas with rocket and remaining coriander mixture.

MISO VEGETABLES WITH POUNDED RICE SALAD

PREP + COOK TIME 30 MINUTES SERVES 4

2 tablespoons sesame oil

4 king brown mushrooms, trimmed, quartered lengthways

170g (5½ ounces) asparagus, trimmed, halved lengthways

6 green onions (scallions), trimmed, sliced thinly

400g (12½ ounces) enoki mushrooms, trimmed

POUNDED RICE SALAD

¼ cup (55g) sushi rice

1 large (350g) yellow capsicum (bell pepper), sliced finely

1 large (350g) red capsicum (bell pepper), sliced finely

½ cup loosely packed coriander (cilantro) leaves

½ cup loosely packed vietnamese mint leaves

1 cup (100g) bean sprouts

2 tablespoons sesame seeds, toasted

MISO SAUCE

¼ cup (60g) white (shiro) miso

¼ cup (60ml) rice vinegar

1 tablespoon honey

1 teaspoon finely chopped pickled ginger

1 tablespoon pickled ginger juice

½ teaspoon dried chilli flakes

1 Make pounded rice salad.

2 Make miso sauce.

3 Heat a wok over medium high heat. Add sesame oil and king brown mushrooms; stir-fry for 5 minutes. Transfer to a tray. Stir-fry asparagus and green onions for 2 minutes; transfer to tray. Stir-fry enoki mushrooms for 30 seconds or until heated through; transfer to tray.

4 Serve vegetables topped with miso sauce and rice salad.

POUNDED RICE SALAD Heat a large frying pan over medium heat, add rice; stir continuously for 4 minutes or until rice is lightly golden and toasted. Grind toasted rice in a mortar and pestle to a fine powder. Place ground rice in a medium bowl with remaining ingredients; stir to combine.

MISO SAUCE Whisk ingredients in a small bowl; season.

Bean curd sheets are available from Asian food stores. If they are hard to find, you could use fresh rice noodle sheets or blanched cabbage leaves instead. Steam as the recipe directs.

VEGETABLE BEAN CURD ROLLS

PREP + COOK TIME 45 MINUTES SERVES 4

50g (1½ ounces) dried rice vermicelli noodles

1 tablespoon sesame oil

200g (6½ ounces) shiitake mushrooms, sliced thinly

100g (3 ounces) enoki mushrooms, trimmed

3 cups (240g) finely shredded wombok (napa cabbage)

200g (6½ ounces) green beans, sliced thinly

1 medium carrot (120g), cut into matchsticks

1 cup (80g) bean sprouts

⅓ cup (80ml) char siu sauce

2 tablespoons tamari or soy sauce

2 tablespoons toasted sesame seeds

4 bean curd sheets (125g) (see Notes)

1 teaspoon cornflour (cornstarch)

1 Place noodles in a small heatproof bowl, cover with boiling water, stand until just tender; drain.

2 Heat oil in a wok over high heat; stir-fry mushrooms for 2 minutes or until golden and tender. Add wombok, beans and carrot; stir-fry for 1 minute or until almost tender. Add sprouts, noodles, 2 tablespoons of the char siu sauce, half the tamari and half the sesame seeds; stir-fry for 30 seconds or until heated through. Drain, reserving cooking liquid.

3 Halve bean curd sheets. Top with ½ cup of the vegetable mixture. Fold sheet over filling, then fold in both sides. Continue rolling to enclose filling. Repeat with remaining vegetable mixture and sheets to make a total of eight rolls.

4 Steam rolls, covered, over a large wok of simmering water for 10 minutes or until bean curd is tender.

5 Meanwhile, whisk cornflour and reserved cooking liquid in a small saucepan until combined. Stir in remaining char siu sauce, tamari and seeds. Place pan over medium-high heat; cook, uncovered, for 5 minutes or until mixture boils and thickens.

6 Serve vegetable rolls with sauce; sprinkle with extra sesame seeds, if you like.

ZUCCHINI & TOFU NOODLES WITH CORIANDER PESTO

PREP + COOK TIME 30 MINUTES SERVES 4

¼ cup (60ml) olive oil

250g (8 ounces) firm tofu, chopped coarsely

250g (8 ounces) yellow patty pan squash, quartered

350g (11 ounces) zucchini, halved lengthways, chopped coarsely

2 teaspoons finely grated fresh ginger

2 cloves garlic, crushed

1 tablespoon light soy sauce

180g (5½ ounces) dried soba noodles

½ cup (75g) roasted cashews, chopped coarsely

1 cup loosely packed fresh coriander (cilantro) leaves (see Note)

CORIANDER PESTO

1 cup (150g) roasted cashews

3 cups loosely packed fresh coriander (cilantro) leaves

1 clove garlic, crushed

2 teaspoons finely grated lemon rind

1 tablespoon lemon juice

1 fresh long green chilli, seeded, chopped coarsely

½ cup (125ml) olive oil

1 Make coriander pesto.

2 Heat 2 tablespoons of the oil in a large deep frying pan over high heat; cook tofu for 3 minutes each side or until golden. Remove from pan; keep warm.

3 Heat remaining oil in same pan; cook squash and zucchini, stirring, for 5 minutes or until golden and tender. Add ginger and garlic; cook, stirring for 30 seconds or until fragrant. Add sauce; cook for 1 minute.

4 Meanwhile, cook noodles in a large saucepan of boiling water, uncovered, until just tender; drain. Return noodles to pan, add pesto; toss to combine.

5 Serve noodles with zucchini mixture and tofu; top with cashews and coriander.

CORIANDER PESTO Blend or process ingredients until smooth; season to taste.

NOTE You will need to buy 3 bunches coriander (cilantro) for this recipe.

You can fill
eggplants ahead
of time; store,
covered in the
refrigerator
until required.
Roast just
before serving.

WALNUT & MISO FILLED EGGPLANT WITH RADISH SALAD

PREP + COOK TIME 50 MINUTES SERVES 4

4 lebanese eggplants (370g)

2 tablespoons olive oil

½ cup (60g) finely chopped walnuts

½ cup (85g) cooked brown basmati rice

2 green onions (scallions), sliced thinly

1 clove garlic, crushed

1 tablespoon white miso paste

2 teaspoons light soy sauce

2 teaspoons mirin

RADISH SALAD

2 lebanese cucumbers (260g), sliced thinly lengthways

250g (8 ounces) red radishes, trimmed, sliced thinly

2 green onions (scallions), sliced thinly lengthways

2 tablespoons rice vinegar

2 teaspoons light soy sauce

¼ teaspoon sesame oil

1 Preheat oven to 180°C/350°F. Line an oven tray with baking paper.

2 Cut eggplants in half lengthways. Score a 5mm (¼-inch) border with a small knife. Spoon out flesh leaving a shell. Coarsely chop flesh. Place eggplant shells on tray.

3 Heat oil in a non-stick large frying pan over high heat; cook chopped eggplant, walnuts, rice, green onion and garlic, stirring, for 5 minutes or until eggplant is tender. Add miso, sauce and mirin; cook, stirring, for 30 seconds or until eggplant is coated. Spoon mixture into eggplant shells.

4 Roast filled eggplant for 25 minutes or until golden and tender.

5 Meanwhile make radish salad.

6 Serve filled eggplant topped with radish salad.

RADISH SALAD Place ingredients in a medium bowl; toss gently to combine.

CHICKPEA 'TOFU' WITH SPICED BLACK-EYED BEANS

PREP + COOK TIME 1 HOUR 30 MINUTES (+ STANDING & REFRIGERATION) SERVES 4

You will need to start this recipe the day before.

1½ cups (300g) black-eyed beans

1 tablespoon olive oil

1 large brown onion (200g), chopped finely

4 cloves garlic, chopped finely

4 teaspoons finely grated fresh ginger

2 tablespoons ground cumin

1 tablespoon sweet paprika

½ teaspoon chilli powder

400g (12½ ounces) canned diced tomatoes

1 cup (250ml) coconut cream

2 teaspoons caster (superfine) sugar

2 tablespoons lemon juice

2 tablespoons olive oil, extra

⅓ cup (50g) chopped cashews, roasted, halved

1 fresh long green chilli, sliced thinly

CHICKPEA 'TOFU'

1 cup (150g) chickpea (besan) flour

2 teaspoons ground cumin

1 teaspoon ground turmeric

1 teaspoon sea salt flakes

3 cups (750ml) water

1 Place beans in a medium bowl, cover with cold water; stand 2 hours. Drain. Rinse under cold water; drain. Place beans in a medium saucepan of boiling water; return to a boil. Reduce heat; simmer, for 1 hour or until beans are tender. Drain.

2 Meanwhile, make chickpea 'tofu'.

3 Heat oil in a large saucepan over medium heat; cook onion, garlic, ginger, cumin, paprika and chilli powder for 5 minutes or until onion softens. Add beans, tomatoes, coconut cream and sugar; cook, stirring occasionally, for 15 minutes or until sauce thickens. Stir in juice; season to taste.

4 Meanwhile, remove chickpea 'tofu' from pan; cut into eight rectangles. Heat extra oil in a large non-stick frying pan over high heat; cook chickpea 'tofu' for 1 minute each side or until golden.

5 Serve chickpea 'tofu' topped with bean mixture, cashews and chilli.

CHICKPEA 'TOFU' Grease and line a 19cm (7¾-inch) square cake pan with baking paper. Combine flour, cumin, turmeric and salt in a medium bowl. Add half the water; whisking, until smooth and combined. Place the remaining water in a medium saucepan over high heat; bring to the boil. Add chickpea mixture; cook, whisking continuously, for 2 minutes or until thick and glossy. Pour mixture into pan. Refrigerate for 2 hours or until set.

VEGAN YOGHURT

PREP + COOK TIME 5 MINUTES

(+ STANDING) MAKES 2½ CUPS

Place 1 cup (150g) cashews and 1 cup (160g) whole blanched almonds in a large bowl; cover with cold water. Stand, covered, for 4 hours or overnight. Drain; rinse under cold water. Drain. Process nuts with 1 cup (250ml) water until it forms a yoghurt-like consistency.

NOTES

You can experiment with different nuts to create this yoghurt, bearing in mind the flavour each nut will create.

Stir in the juice of 1 lemon for a great savoury yoghurt option to add to salads or top soups and curries.

Store vegan yoghurt in the fridge for up to 1 week.

VEGAN PASSIONFRUIT YOGHURT

Make vegan yoghurt opposite; stir in the pulp of 3 passionfruit.

VEGAN STRAWBERRY YOGHURT

Make vegan yoghurt opposite using 1 cup (150g) cashews and 1 cup (120g) pecans. Blend or process 250g (8 ounces) strawberries until smooth. Fold strawberry puree through yoghurt to create a swirled effect.

Finding a good-quality vegan mayonnaise is difficult and most are soy based. This recipe is not only dairy-free and egg-free, but soy-free as well.

VEGAN MAYONNAISE

10 MINUTES (+ STANDING)

MAKES 2 CUPS

Soak 1 cup (160g) whole blanched almonds for 4 hours; drain. Rinse under cold water; drain. Blend almonds with ½ cup (125ml) water until smooth. Add 1 tablespoon apple cider vinegar, 1 tablespoon lemon juice and 1 teaspoon dijon mustard; blend until smooth and combined. Season to taste. With motor operating, add ½ cup (125ml) olive oil in a slow, steady stream until smooth and combined. Store in an airtight container in the fridge for up to 1 month.

VEGAN LEMON & PEPPER MAYONNAISE

Make vegan mayonnaise opposite; stir in 2 teaspoons finely grated lemon rind and ½ teaspoon ground black pepper.

Test Kitchen NOTES

If the vegan mayonnaise is not tart enough for your taste, add a little more lemon juice. If it is too tart, add a little cold water.

Spread these mayonnaises on sandwiches, serve as an accompaniment with vegan recipes, as an ingredient in place of egg-based mayonnaise, or as a dip with vegetable sticks.

VEGAN HARISSA MAYONNAISE

Make vegan mayonnaise (see page 108); stir in harissa to taste.

VEGAN AIOLI

Make vegan mayonnaise
(see page 108); stir in
1 clove crushed garlic.

COOKING TECHNIQUES

TRIMMING BEETROOT

To trim beetroot, cut the stems to 2cm (¾ inch) from the bulb. Don't trim the beard at the base of the plant as this stops the colour from bleeding during cooking.

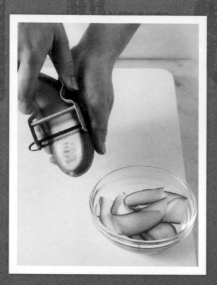

SLICING CUCUMBER

Slicing cucumbers into ribbons will give thin, uniform slices. The best tool for this is a vegetable peeler. Applying more pressure on the peeler gives thicker ribbons.

WASHING A LEEK

To wash a leek, cut it in half lengthwise, stopping at the root. Fan the layers out and wash under fast-running cold water. This removes any grit from the inside layers.

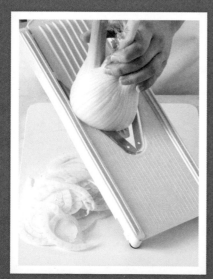

SLICING FENNEL

Slicing fennel thinly is easy using a V-slicer or mandoline – simply slide the fennel back and forth across the blade. The adjustable blade is very sharp, so watch your fingers. A guard is supplied, so use it to protect your fingers from any unwanted mishaps.

SEEDING A POMEGRANATE

Cut the pomegranate in half and hold it over a bowl. Hit it sharply with a spoon – the seeds (surrounded by the pulp) should fall out – if they don't, dig them out with a teaspoon. Be careful, as the pomegranate juice can stain your hands, clothes and bench top

CUTTING ONION WEDGES

Cut the onion in half lengthways through the root. Remove the papery outer skin. Lie the onion cut-side down and cut the onion lengthways through the root into triangular-shaped wedges. The root holds the wedges together.

SLICING CAPSICUM

To slice a capsicum, cut the top and bottom off and stand it on one end; slice down removing all the flesh. Remove and discard the seeds and membranes, then slice the flesh.

ZESTING CITRUS FRUIT

A zester has very small, and very sharp, holes that cut the rind (the outermost layer of the fruit) into thin ribbons but leaves the bitter pith (the white layer) behind.

MAKE A THIN OMELETTE

To make a thin omelette, lightly whisk the eggs, then pour into a heated lightly-oiled wok (or large frying pan). Tilt the wok to cover the base with the egg; cook until the egg is set.

HOW TO CHIFFONADE

Chiffonade is a way of cutting green leaves into long, thin strips. Lay leaves flat on top of each other, then roll up tightly and cut into thin slices.

TOASTING NUTS

Regardless of the type of nut, toasting them is the same. Stir nuts over a low heat in a dry frying pan until golden brown. Remove the nuts immediately from the pan to stop them burning.

CRUSHING GARLIC

Press garlic firmly with the flat blade of a large knife (top) crushing the clove. Pull off the papery skin and finely chop the clove. A garlic press (bottom) removes and leaves the skin behind while crushing the garlic.

GLOSSARY

ARTICHOKES

globe large flower-bud member of the thistle family; it has tough petal-like leaves, and is edible in part when cooked.

hearts the tender centre of the globe artichoke; purchased, in brine, canned or in glass jars.

BAMBOO SHOOTS the tender shoots of bamboo plants, available in cans; must be rinsed and drained before use.

BARLEY a nutritious grain used in soups and stews. Hulled barley, the least processed, is high in fibre. Pearl barley has had the husk removed then been steamed and polished so that only the 'pearl' of the original grain remains, much the same as white rice.

BEANS

borlotti also called roman beans or pink beans; available both fresh and dried. Interchangeable with pinto beans due to their similarity in appearance – pale pink or beige with dark red streaks.

broad (fava) also called windsor and horse beans; available dried, fresh, canned and frozen. Fresh should be peeled twice (discarding the outer long green pod and the beige-green tough inner shell); frozen beans have had their pods removed but the beige shell still needs removal.

butter also known as lima beans; large, flat, kidney-shaped bean, off-white in colour, with a mild taste. Available canned and dried, and fresh in the pod.

cannellini a small white bean similar in appearance and flavour to other white beans (great northern, navy or haricot), all of which can be substituted for the other. Available dried or canned.

edamame are fresh green baby soya beans; They are available, fresh and frozen, from major supermarkets and Asian grocery stores.

kidney medium-sized red bean, slightly floury in texture, yet sweet in flavour.

sprouts also known as bean shoots; tender new growths of assorted beans and seeds germinated for consumption.

white a generic term we use for canned or dried cannellini, haricot, navy or great northern beans. All these beans are of the same family and can be substituted for the other.

BEETROOT (beets) also known as red beets; a firm, round root vegetable.

BREADCRUMBS, PANKO (japanese) are available in two types: larger pieces and fine crumbs. Both have a lighter texture than Western-style breadcrumbs. They are at all Asian grocery stores and, unless you make rather coarse breadcrumbs from white bread that's either quite stale or gently toasted, nothing is an adequate substitute. Has a crunchy texture with a delicate, pale golden colour.

BROCCOLINI a cross between broccoli and chinese kale; long asparagus-like stems with a long loose floret, both completely edible. Resembles broccoli but is milder and sweeter in taste.

BUK CHOY also known as bok choy, pak choi, chinese white cabbage or chinese chard; has a fresh, mild mustard taste. Use both stems and leaves. Baby buk choy, also known as pak kat farang or shanghai bok choy, is smaller and more tender than buk choy.

BUTTER use salted or unsalted (sweet) butter; 125g is equal to one stick of butter (4 ounces).

CAPERS grey-green buds of a warm climate shrub (usually Mediterranean); sold dried and salted or pickled in a vinegar brine. *Baby capers*, those picked early, are very small, fuller-flavoured and more expensive than the full-size ones. Capers, whether packed in brine or in salt, must be rinsed well before using.

CAPSICUM (bell pepper) also known as just 'pepper'. Comes in many colours: red, green, yellow, orange and purplish-black. Be sure to discard seeds and membranes before use.

CELERIAC (celery root) tuberous root with knobbly brown skin, white flesh and a celery-like flavour. Keep peeled celeriac in acidulated water (water with lemon juice in it) to stop it discolouring. It can be grated and eaten raw in salads; used in soups and stews; boiled and mashed like potatoes; or sliced thinly and deep-fried.

CHEESE

cream cheese known as Philadelphia or Philly; a soft, cows'-milk cheese sold at supermarkets. Also available as a spreadable light cream cheese – a blend of cottage and cream cheeses.

fetta Greek in origin; a crumbly textured goat- or sheep-milk cheese having a sharp, salty taste. Ripened and stored in salted whey.

fetta, persian a soft, creamy fetta marinated in a blend of olive oil, garlic, herbs and spices. It is available from most larger supermarkets.

goat's made from goats' milk; it has an earthy taste. Is available in both soft and firm textures, in various shapes and sizes, and sometimes rolled in ash or herbs.

gorgonzola a creamy blue cheese with a mild, sweet taste.

haloumi a firm, cream-coloured sheep-milk cheese matured in brine; haloumi can be grilled or fried, briefly, without breaking down. Should be eaten while still warm as it becomes tough and rubbery on cooling.

mascarpone a cultured cream product made in much the same way as yoghurt. Is whitish to creamy yellow in colour, with a soft, creamy texture and a rich, sweet, slightly acidic, taste.

mozzarella soft, spun-curd cheese. It originated in southern Italy where it was traditionally made from water-buffalo milk. Now, generally made from cows' milk, it is the most popular pizza cheese because of its low melting point and elasticity when heated.

parmesan also called parmigiano; this hard, grainy cows'-milk cheese originated in Italy. Reggiano is the best variety.

pecorino the generic Italian name for cheeses made from sheep milk; hard, white to pale-yellow cheeses. If you can't find it, use parmesan.

ricotta a soft, sweet, moist, white cows'-milk cheese with a low fat content and a slightly grainy texture. The name roughly translates as 'cooked again' and refers to ricotta's manufacture from whey, which is itself a by-product of other cheese making.

CHICKPEAS (garbanzo beans) also called hummus or channa; an irregularly round, sandy-coloured legume. They remain firm after cooking, with a floury mouth-feel and robust nutty flavour; available canned or dried (reconstitute for several hours in cold water before use).

CHILLI generally, the smaller the chilli, the hotter it is. Use rubber gloves when seeding and chopping fresh chillies as they can burn your skin. Removing seeds and membranes lessens the heat level.

long available both fresh and dried; a generic term used for any moderately hot, long (6-8cm/2¼-3¼ inch), thin chilli.

red thai small, hot and bright red. Substitute with fresh serrano chillies.

CHINESE COOKING WINE (shao hsing) also known as chinese rice wine; made from fermented rice, wheat, sugar and salt with a 13.5% alcohol content. Inexpensive and found in Asian food shops and supermarkets; if you can't find it, replace with mirin or sherry.

CINNAMON available in pieces (called sticks or quills) and ground into powder; one of the world's most common spices, used as a sweet, fragrant flavouring for both sweet and savoury foods.

COCONUT

cream obtained commercially from the first pressing of the coconut flesh alone, without the addition of water. Available in cans and cartons at most supermarkets.

desiccated concentrated, unsweetened, dried and finely shredded coconut flesh.

milk not the liquid found inside the fruit (coconut water), but the diluted liquid from the second pressing of the white flesh of a mature coconut (the first pressing produces coconut cream).

CORIANDER (cilantro) also known as pak chee or chinese parsley; a bright-green leafy herb with a pungent flavour. Both the stems and roots of coriander are also used; wash well before using. Also available ground or as seeds; these should not be substituted for fresh coriander as the tastes are completely different.

COUSCOUS a fine, grain-like cereal product made from semolina; it swells to three or four times its original size when liquid is added.

CREAM

pouring also known as pure, fresh or single cream. It has no additives and contains a minimum fat content of 35%.

thickened (heavy) a whipping cream that contains a thickener. It has a minimum fat content of 35%.

CUMIN a spice also known as zeera or comino; has a spicy, nutty flavour.

CURRY LEAVES available fresh or dried and have a mild curry flavour.

CURRY PASTES commercially made pastes vary in strengths and flavours. Use whichever one you feel best suits your spice-level tolerance.

green the hottest of the traditional pastes; contains chilli, garlic, onion, salt, lemon grass, spices and galangal.

massaman rich, spicy flavour reminiscent of Middle-Eastern cooking; favoured by southern Thai cooks for use in hot and sour stew-like curries and satay sauces.

penang based on the curries of Penang, an island off the north-west coast of Malaysia, close to the Thai border. A complex, sweet and milder variation of red curry paste; good with seafood and for adding to soups and salad dressings.

red a popular curry paste; a hot blend of red chilli, garlic, shallot, lemon grass, salt, galangal, shrimp paste, kaffir lime peel, coriander, cumin and paprika. It is milder than the hotter thai green paste.

EGGPLANT also known as aubergine. Ranging in size from tiny to very large and in colour from pale green to deep purple. May also be purchased char-grilled, packed in oil, in jars.

FENNEL also known as finocchio or anise; a white to very pale green-white, firm, crisp, roundish vegetable about 8-12cm in diameter. The bulb has a slightly sweet, anise flavour but the leaves have a much stronger taste. Also the name given to the dried seeds, which have a licorice flavour.

FLOUR

atta a fine wholemeal flour used for Indian flatbreads. It is available from most major supermarkets and Indian food stores.

plain a general all-purpose wheat flour.

self-raising (self-rising) plain flour sifted with baking powder in the proportion of 1 cup flour to 2 teaspoons baking powder.

wholemeal also known as wholewheat flour; milled with the wheat germ intact so is higher in fibre and more nutritional than plain flour.

GAI LAN also known as chinese broccoli, gai larn, kanah, gai lum and chinese kale; appreciated more for its stems than its coarse leaves.

GARAM MASALA a blend of spices that includes cardamom, cinnamon, fennel, coriander, cloves and cumin. Black pepper and chilli can be added for heat.

KAFFIR LIME LEAVES also known as bai magrood. Aromatic leaves of a citrus tree; two glossy dark green leaves joined end to end, forming a rounded hourglass shape. A strip of fresh lime peel may be substituted for each kaffir lime leaf.

KECAP MANIS a thick soy sauce with added sugar and spices. The sweetness is derived from the addition of molasses or palm sugar.

KUMARA (orange sweet potato) the Polynesian name of an orange-fleshed sweet potato often confused with yam.

LABNE is a soft cheese made by salting plain (natural) yoghurt and draining it of whey for up to 2 days until it becomes thick enough to roll into small balls. These may be sprinkled with or rolled in chopped herbs or spices.

LEBANESE CUCUMBER short, slender and thin-skinned. Probably the most popular variety because of its tender, edible skin, tiny, yielding seeds and sweet, fresh flavoursome taste.

LEEK a member of the onion family, the leek resembles a green onion but is much larger and more subtle in flavour. Tender baby or pencil leeks can be eaten whole with minimal cooking, but adult leeks are usually trimmed of most of the green tops then chopped or sliced.

LEMON GRASS a tall, clumping, lemon-smelling and -tasting, sharp-edged grass; the white lower part of the stem is used, finely chopped, in cooking.

LENTILS (red, brown, yellow) dried pulses often identified by and named after their colour; also known as dhal.

french-style green lentils are a local cousin to the famous (and expensive) French lentils du puy; green-blue, tiny lentils with a nutty, earthy flavour and a hardy nature that allows them to be rapidly cooked without disintegrating.

yellow also called channa dhal, are available from specialty stores and Indian food shops. They are not commonly found in supermarkets.

MUSHROOMS

enoki clumps of long, spaghetti-like stems with tiny, snowy white caps.

flat large, flat mushrooms with a rich earthy flavour. They are sometimes misnamed field mushrooms, which are wild mushrooms.

oyster also known as abalone; these grey-white mushrooms shaped like a fan. They are prized for their smooth texture and subtle, oyster-like flavour.

portobello are mature, fully opened swiss browns; they are larger in size, and stronger in flavour.

shiitake when fresh are also called chinese black, forest or golden oak mushrooms; although cultivated, they are large and meaty and have the earthiness and taste of wild mushrooms. When dried, they are called donko or dried chinese mushrooms; rehydrate before use.

swiss brown also known as cremini or roman mushrooms, are light brown mushrooms having a full-bodied flavour.

MUSTARD SEEDS are available in black, brown or yellow varieties. Available from supermarkets and health-food shops.

ONIONS

green (scallions) also known, incorrectly, as shallot; an immature onion picked before the bulb has formed. Has a long, bright-green edible stalk.

shallots also called french shallots, golden shallots or eschalots; small, brown-skinned, elongated members of the onion family.

spring have small white bulbs and long, narrow, green-leafed tops.

POLENTA also known as cornmeal; a flour-like cereal made of ground corn (maize). Also the name of the dish that is made from it.

POMEGRANATE dark-red, leathery-skinned fresh fruit about the size of an orange filled with hundreds of seeds, each wrapped in an edible lucent-crimson pulp having a unique tangy sweet-sour flavour.

POMEGRANATE MOLASSES not to be confused with pomegranate syrup or grenadine (which is used in cocktails); pomegranate molasses is thicker, browner and more concentrated in flavour – tart, sharp, slightly sweet and fruity. Buy it from Middle-Eastern food stores or specialty food shops.

PRESERVED LEMON RIND a North African specialty; lemons are quartered and preserved in salt and lemon juice or water. To use, remove and discard the pulp, squeeze the juice from the rind, rinse the rind well, then slice thinly.

QUINOA pronounced 'keen-wa'; is a gluten-free grain. It has a delicate, slightly nutty taste and chewy texture. Its cooking qualities are similar to rice. It spoils easily, so keep sealed in the fridge.

RADICCHIO a red-leafed Italian chicory, with a bitter taste, eaten raw and grilled. Comes in varieties that are named after their places of origin, such as round-headed Verona or long-headed Treviso.

RAS EL HANOUT a classic spice blend used in Moroccan cooking. The name means 'top of the shop' and is the very best spice blend a spice merchant has to offer. Most versions contain over a dozen spices, including cardamom, nutmeg, mace, cinnamon and ground chilli.

RICE

arborio small, round grain rice well-suited to absorb a large amount of liquid; the high level of starch makes it especially suitable for risottos.

wild not a member of the rice family but the seed of an aquatic grass native to the cold regions of North America. Wild rice has a strong nutty taste and can be expensive, so is best combined with other rices.

SAFFRON available ground or in strands; imparts a yellow-orange colour to food. The quality can vary greatly; the best is the most expensive spice in the world.

SAMBAL OELEK (also ulek or olek) Indonesian in origin; a salty paste made from ground chillies and vinegar. Found in supermarkets and Asian food stores.

SILVER BEET also known as swiss chard and blettes; may also mistakenly be called spinach. Grown for its tasty green leaves and celery-like stems.

SNOW PEAS also called mange tout ('eat all'). *Snow pea tendrils*, the growing shoots of the plant, are also available at greengrocers. *Snow pea sprouts* are the tender new growths of snow peas.

SPINACH also known as english spinach and, incorrectly, silver beet.

SPLIT PEAS a variety of yellow or green pea grown specifically for drying. When dried, the peas usually split along a natural seam.

SUMAC a purple-red, astringent spice ground from berries growing on shrubs in the Mediterranean; adds a tart, lemony flavour to food. Available from spice shops and major supermarkets.

TAHINI a rich sesame-seed paste.

VINEGAR

balsamic originally from Modena, Italy, there are now many balsamic vinegars on the market ranging in pungency and quality depending on how, and for how long, they have been aged. Quality can be determined up to a point by price; use the most expensive sparingly.

glaze a reduction of balsamic vinegar; also called crema or balsamic reduction; has no added sugar or preservatives.

white made from spirit of cane sugar.

WATER CHESTNUT resembles a chestnut in appearance, hence the English name. They are small brown tubers with a crisp, white, nutty-tasting flesh. Their crunchy texture is best experienced fresh, however, canned chestnuts are more easily obtained.

WATERCRESS a member of the cress family, a large group of peppery greens. Highly perishable, so must be used as soon as possible after purchase.

WOMBOK (napa cabbage) also known as peking cabbage, chinese cabbage or petsai; elongated in shape with pale green, crinkly leaves.

ZA'ATAR a Middle Eastern herb and spice mixture which varies in makeup; however, it always includes thyme, ground sumac and, usually, toasted sesame seeds.

ZUCCHINI also called courgette; a small, pale- or dark-green or yellow vegetable.

INDEX

This book is published in 2015 by Octopus Publishing Group Limited
based on materials licensed to it by Bauer Media Books, Australia
Bauer Media Books is a division of Bauer Media Pty Limited.
54 Park St, Sydney; GPO Box 4088, Sydney, NSW 2001, Australia
phone (+61) 2 9282 8618; fax (+61) 2 9126 3702
www.awwcookbooks.com.au

MEDIA GROUP
BAUER MEDIA BOOKS
Publisher – Jo Runciman
Editorial & food director – Pamela Clark
Director of sales, marketing & rights – Brian Cearnes
Creative director – Hieu Nguyen
Art director – Hannah Blackmore
Senior editor – Kyle Rankin
Food editor – Sophia Young

Published and Distributed in the United Kingdom by Octopus Publishing Group
Carmelite House
50 Victoria Embankment
London EC4Y 0DZ
phone (+44) (0) 207 632 5400; fax (+44) (0) 207 632 5405
info@octopus-publishing.co.uk;
www.octopusbooks.co.uk

Printed by Toppan Printing Co., China

International foreign language rights, Brian Cearnes, Bauer Media Books
bcearnes@bauer-media.com.au

A catalogue record for this book is available from the British Library.
ISBN: 978 1909770 256 (paperback)
© Bauer Media Pty Ltd 2015
ABN 18 053 273 546

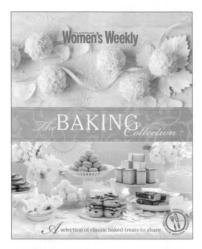
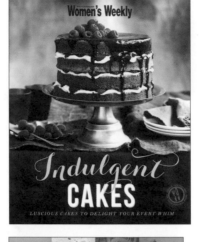

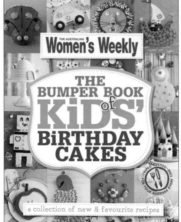
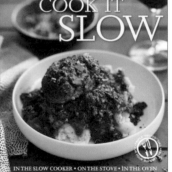